Mantle
Remembered

Sports Illustrated Presents

Mantle
Remembered

Stories excerpted from the pages of *Sports Illustrated*
Original text by Robert W. Creamer

WARNER BOOKS
A Time Warner Company

Warner Books, Inc., 1271 Avenue of the
Americas, New York, New York 10020

 A Time Warner Company

Printed in the United States of America

First Printing: November 1995

10   9   8   7   6   5   4   3   2   1

ISBN: 0-446-52062-4
LC: 95-61862

Mantle Remembered was produced by
Bishop Books of New York City.

Cover photograph: Art Rickerby
Back cover photograph: Mark Kauffman/Life

Mantle Remembered

American Icon

During his final illness and after his death Mickey Mantle was referred to repeatedly as

an American "icon." The constant repetition of "icon" bothered me. I knew that originally the word had religious significance in the Eastern Orthodox Church, but I didn't see how it could properly be applied to a ballplayer.

In my ignorance I went to the dictionary. The religious definition was there, of course, but I learned that an icon can also be "an enduring symbol." It can be "the object of great attention and devotion." An icon can be an "idol."

I understood then, finally, that Mickey Mantle was indeed an American icon, something that other splendid players of his era were not. Not Stan Musial, probably the best all-around player of Mantle's era. Not Willie Mays. Not Henry Aaron or Roberto Clemente. Not even the fabulous Ted Williams aroused the widespread awe and affection that enfolded Mantle and grew and grew in the years after he left the game. Mantle truly became an enduring symbol of his era.

Why is this? How did this hard-drinking, fun-loving boy from Oklahoma become an idol? Part of the reason lies in the remarkable fact that in his first fourteen seasons in the big leagues Mantle's Yankees won twelve pennants. He was in the World Series *12* times in 14 years. Autumn after autumn he was on not just a local but a national stage. Ted Williams was in only one World Series, Aaron and Clemente two, Musial in four (all of them in his early seasons before television took over). Mays was in four later on, but they were scattered over 23 years.

Mantle in the Series was like a long-running hit television show. In 1952 at the age of 20 he hit two home runs in the World Series, and a year later he hit two more, including a grand slam. In 1955 he started only two games because of injuries but hit another home run during his brief appearance. He hit three homers in the 1956 Series, three in '60 and three in '64. In all, he hit 18 Series home runs, obliterating Babe Ruth's old record of 15. Long before Reggie

by Robert W. Creamer

Jackson became Mr. October, Mantle was the very epitome of World Series power.

Another key to understanding Mantle's hold on America's affections can be found in the 1964 Series, Mantle's last, when despite his three home runs, his eight runs batted in and his eight runs scored, the Yankees lost. Such failure (if not being able to keep his team from losing can be called a failure) endeared him to the public. He was vulnerable. We sometimes seem to save our greatest devotion for those heroes who don't quite make it, or who lose gallantly, or who have flaws. Mantle more than fit the image.

From the very beginning of his career he seemed oddly fragile, even when he arrived in the New York Yankees' training camp in 1951 looking like the beau ideal of the "phenom" rookie—a 19-year-old country boy, shy and naive, built like a tank with the speed of a racehorse. "This boy hits balls over buildings," marveled the Yankee manager, Casey Stengel. "He runs as fast as Ty Cobb."

But the phenom was imperfect. He had osteomyelitis, an inflammation of bone and bone marrow, and his legs were suspect. He was exempted from military service during the Korean War because of his ailment. Hodgkin's disease was prevalent in his family; it was said that no male in his family had lived past 40. He

was flawed on the field too. In his rookie season with the Yankees he struck out so often that he was returned to the minor leagues for a while. Back with the Yankees he damaged his knee in the second game of the 1951 World Series and played no more that year.

He incurred injuries throughout his career and they seemed to stay with him, further bolstering his image as the gallant hero who valiantly continued to play in pain. When he sprinted at top speed he was as smooth as stainless steel, but when he slowed to a jog, trotting on or off the field, he seemed to move awkwardly, looking, one sportswriter said, as though his feet hurt.

Mantle was the heir apparent to Joe DiMaggio, who retired after Mantle's rookie season, but at first he wasn't able to fill DiMaggio's shoes. It was five years before he really establised himself, and even then he was oddly inconsistent. He hit home runs but over three seasons his batting average fell from .365 to .275—and then soared upward 42 points again the following year. His home run total went up 15 one year, dropped 18 the next. For all his prowess through his first seasons he made Yankee fans uneasy, and he was often booed.

Not until 1961 was he fully accepted. That was the year his teammate Roger Maris hit 61 home runs to break Ruth's single-season

Mantle was fragile from the start; his injury in the '51 Series was the first of many.

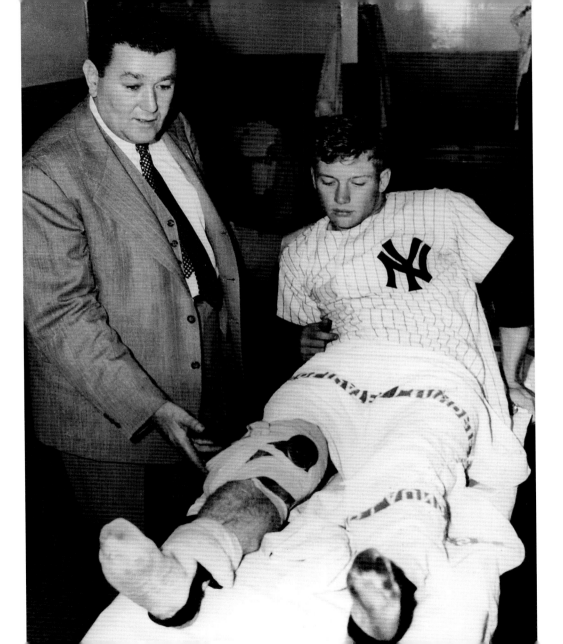

record; Mantle went head-to-head with Maris until a leg injury disabled him late in the season, and he finished with 54. Maris, a relative newcomer, was cast as the upstart villain in the pursuit of Ruth, while Mantle, in his eleventh season, became the darling of the crowd. He was theirs at last, the legitimate successor to Ruth and Lou Gehrig and DiMaggio.

In 1962 he missed nearly 40 games but even so won the Most Valuable Player award (for the third time). He missed more than half the season in 1963 but came back in '64 to have one of his best years, including his valiant effort in the Series. He played four more years after that, but they were sad times. His legs were gone, and the Yankee dynasty was gone too. The club fell into the doldrums it has remained in, with few exceptions, for three decades. Mantle's final season was 1968, the last year before baseball split its two major leagues into divisions and introduced multi-team postseason playoffs. Thus, Mantle's last year in baseball marked the end of an era, literally.

Nostalgia, longing for the past, enriched his fame in retirement. Middle-aged fans too young to have seen DiMaggio play had grown up watching Mickey. He was *their* man, their symbol of times past. When he appeared at Old-timers games in Yankee Stadium and else-where, the cheers were passionate with longing for the days when he was Mickey Mantle and the world was young.

Unlike DiMaggio, Mantle in retirement became affable and open. He was on television a lot. He was the subject of several books. He was generous with interviews. His easy south-western accent was pleasing, and so was his face, handsomer than when he was young. He told stories well. People watching and listening felt they knew him, that he was an old friend.

He was still imperfect. He hustled for money, did commercials, made publicity appearances, fronted for the restaurant that bears his name, signed autographs at card shows. Stories about his excessive partying began to spread. Mantle talked openly and engagingly about his escapades until, finally, he realized what the drinking and high living had done to his body. He was honest about that too, and this time more serious, admitting to alcoholism and what it had done to him and his family. Instead of losing friends and admirers because of the admission, his candor gained him more.

In his final inning on earth he handled himself the way a brave man should, the way his fans and friends expected him to, without bitterness or complaint. He was Mickey Mantle to the end, an imperfect hero, but the icon of an age.

Flawed but powerful: Dodging the fans after beating Chicago with a 10th inning homer in 1959.

The Early Years

1951–1956

Yankee Stadium • 1956

Mickey Mantle was born in Oklahoma
in the depths of the Depression, on October 20, 1931.

His father was a miner, and Mantle might have followed the same career if it had not been for baseball.

He was ten when the U.S. entered World War II and only 13 and about to enter high school when it ended in August, 1945. In high school he developed into an extraordinarily talented athlete, and when he graduated in 1949 he signed a contract to play pro baseball. He had grown up rooting for the St. Louis Cardinals, but the team he signed with was the New York Yankees, who paid him an $1,100 bonus.

In his first minor league season, still only 17, he hit .313 for Independence, Kansas, in the Kansas-Oklahoma-Missouri League and in 1950 was promoted to the farm club at Joplin, Missouri in the Western Association. There he led the league with a .383 average, hit 26 homers and drove in 136 runs. He made such an impression that in 1951 the Yankees invited him to an "instructional school" for promising minor leaguers, held before regular spring training began.

Mantle had been a shortstop at Independence and Joplin, but he made 47 errors his first year and 55 his second and the Yankees switched him to the outfield. They were so impressed by the youngster's power at bat, his speed on the bases and his powerful throwing arm that they kept him with the parent club and he opened the 1951 season with the Yankees, a big leaguer at 19.

He may have been in the majors, but he was still a young, bewildered boy. When he was sent back to the minors in mid-season for a little retooling he called home and told his father he was thinking of quitting. In later years Mantle often told the story of his father visiting him in his minor league hotel. Mickey expected sympathy but received none. Instead, the elder Mantle began packing his son's clothes. When the bewildered boy asked what he was doing the father said, as Mickey told it in his southwestern accent, "Yer a quitter. Yer nothing but a carrid. I'm taking you home. You can go to work in the mines."

A chastened Mantle hit .361 in the minors and returned to the Yankees before the 1951 season was over, this time to stay. Yet it remained a trying time for him. He started in the World Series

by Robert W. Creamer

14

that October, leading off and playing right field, but in the second game he fell in the outfield trying to avoid a collision with center fielder Joe DiMaggio and damaged his knee. Then he discovered that his father was ill with cancer; the elder Mantle died before the next season began. DiMaggio retired after the 1951 World Series, and Mantle was given his spot in center field and expected to take over his role as Yankee leader, too. But that was too much to expect. Mantle occasionally did extraordinary things, like hitting a 565-foot home run in 1953 in Washington's Griffith Stadium, the first "tape-measure" home run, but for three seasons he was just a good and occasionally brilliant young player, not another DiMaggio.

Finally, in 1956 he put it all together. That other New York youngster, Willie Mays, had won the home run crown in 1955 with 51. Only six men before Mays had hit 50 homers in a season. Now, as though to show Mays, Mantle hit 52 homers, beat out Ted Williams for the American League batting title and led the league in runs batted in. He had achieved that rare distinction, the Triple Crown.

Never mind about DiMaggio anymore. Never mind about Babe Ruth. Mantle had arrived.

Mantle's mighty uppercut produced a pair of home runs in the 1953 World Series against Brooklyn.

From SI: June 18, 1956

Breakfast with Mickey

by Joan Flynn Dreyspool

By the time Sports Illustrated's Joan Flynn Dreyspool sat down at the breakfast table with Mickey Mantle in June of 1956, the Yankee star had hit 21 home runs, just one less than the all-time mark at that point of the season, set by Babe Ruth in 1928. Mantle had enjoyed five solid seasons in the majors, including his personal high of 37 home runs in '55, but his burst of tape-measure shots at the beginning of '56 was the first indicator of the greatness that was to come. By the close of the '56 season, Mantle would achieve the triple crown and shed forever the onerous comparisons with Joe DiMaggio, the legend who preceded him in center field.

"This record I've got here now," Mickey Mantle said as he waited for the cantaloupe, buckwheat cakes, sausage, milk and coffee he had ordered in the dining room of his New York hotel, "if you don't keep adding to it, it won't mean anything. It's not even for sure I'll keep on doing it. You can't brag about something like that until the season's over ... and then—" he shrugged his huge shoulders almost helpless-ly—"and then there's next year to worry about.

"I like to do good and whenever I'm doing good, I'm happy," the super-slugging switch-hitter said, nervously twisting the gold wedding ring on his left hand. "I really like baseball. I like to play it. When I'm going bad, I'm like everybody else. I'm playing for the money. I love to play baseball when I'm hitting, but when I'm not hitting, it's just work."

"You've matured," he was told. "There are lots of big hitters you can't even talk to after a hitless game."

He squirmed self-consciously in his chair, then when he realized the compliment was sincerely offered, he allowed himself a pleased boyish grin.

"This will be my eighth year in baseball. If you're not adjusted in eight years, then you'll never be.

"I've had a lot of people tell me I was conceited—like if you leave a ballpark after you get beat 1 to 0—well, there'll be 75 or 80 kids pulling at your clothes and asking for autographs, and you don't sign any because you can't sign them all, and then there'll be four or

The great DiMaggio (left) presented Mantle with an exceedingly tough act to follow.

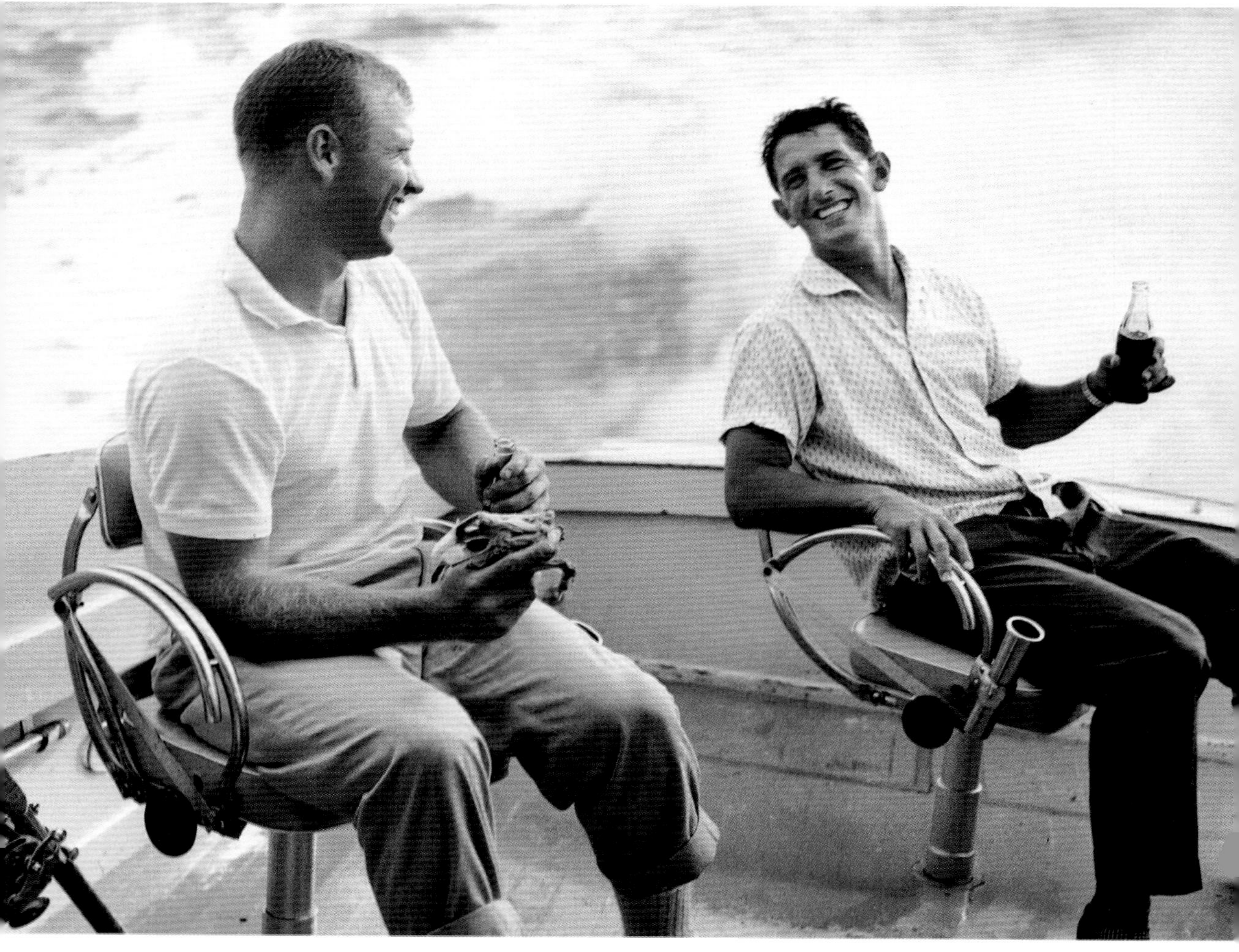

five guys there saying, 'Sign the autographs, you bullheaded bum!'

"They don't understand," he said sadly, "they don't understand."

It is perhaps part of Mantle's developing maturity that he has reconciled himself to the publicity requisites of his profession. Yet he has turned down thousands of dollars' worth of television appearances, restricting himself to only a few shows.

"Baseball is all I've ever been told," he explained. "My dad was a frustrated ballplayer, and even before I was born he named me 'Mickey' after his favorite player, Mickey Cochrane. Then when I was about six months old, I guess, my mother made me my first baseball suit."

Mantle spied his roommate, Billy Martin, and called him over to the table.

"Billy roomed with DiMaggio before DiMaggio left," he said by way of introduction. "After that, we roomed together."

"I live only with big hitters," Martin quipped impishly. " 'Say, there's Joe DiMaggio!' someone would say. 'Who's the guy with him' ... 'Oh, him, just one of the kids on the ball club.' They still say it," he laughed, looking proudly at Mantle.

"Does it bother you always being compared to DiMaggio and trying to live up to the responsibility of it?" Mantle was asked.

"It has never bothered me being compared to DiMaggio," Mantle said thoughtfully. "I never had played outfield before, and I'm still making a lot of bad plays in the outfield that I'll have to correct. I tried to do it, to live up to DiMaggio. It didn't work. I've quit trying now."

"Was it that you were trying to live up to DiMaggio's job or was it that you were trying to do a good job?" Billy Martin put it to his friend. "You weren't conscious of trying to duplicate the things that DiMaggio was doing, were you? You were just trying to do a good job."

Speechlessly grateful, Mantle nodded. "It's when you don't compare yourself to somebody else, or try to do better, that's when you do better," the powerful hitter said from the depths of his new-found maturity. "DiMaggio was the man who could do everything right. There wasn't a thing he couldn't do. I still throw to the wrong base a lot, and," he added apologetically, "I drop fly balls. DiMaggio never did that....

"I'd love to be a fielder like DiMaggio was." Awe had crept into his voice.

Pitcher Tommy Byrne came over to the table. "Come on, Mickey," he said, "we've got to go to the ball park...."

Mantle called for the check and paid it. At the door a starry-eyed waitress rushed up with a handful of menus for Mickey to autograph. He was late already, but he signed.

He doesn't like to be called a bullheaded bum.

19

Mantle and roomie Martin (right): teammates on the field and lifelong friends off it.

From SI: June 18, 1956

The Mantle of the Babe

by Robert W. Creamer

As Mantle's skein of home runs continued in 1956, the whispering began: Is this the man to surpass the legendary Babe Ruth's single-season mark of 60? Mantle would fall short that year, but his total of 52 would forever place the powerful Yankee star in the company of the game's most celebrated power hitters. Sports Illustrated's Robert W. Creamer was one of the first to examine Mantle's prodigious home run capacity.

A thick-bodied, pleasant-faced young man, carrying a bat, stood at home plate in Yankee Stadium, turned the blond bullet head on his bull's neck toward Pedro Ramos, a pitcher in the employ of the Washington Senators, watched intently the flight of the baseball thrown toward him, bent his knees, dropped his right shoulder slightly toward the ball, clenched his bat and raised it to a near-perfect perpendicular. Twisting his massive torso under the guidance of a magnificently tuned set of reflexes, Mickey Mantle so controlled the exorbitant strength generated by his legs, back, shoulders and arms that he brought his bat through the plane of the flight of the pitch with a precision which propelled the ball immensely high and far toward the right-field roof, so high and far that old-timers in the crowd—thinking perhaps of Babe Ruth—watched in awe and held their breath.

For no one had ever hit a fair ball over the majestic height of the gray-green façade that looms above the three tiers of grandstand seats in this, the greatest of ball parks.

Indeed, in the 33 years since the Stadium was opened not one of the great company of home run hitters who have batted there—the list includes Babe Ruth, Lou Gehrig, Joe DiMaggio, Jimmy Foxx, Hank Greenberg and about everyone else you can think of—had even come close to hitting a fair ball over the giant-sized filigree hanging from the lip of the stands which in both right and left field hook far into fair territory toward the bleachers.

Mantle hit the filigree. He came so close to making history that he made it.

The ball struck high on the façade, barely a foot or two below the edge of the roof. Ever

Coiled, concentrated, intense: Mantle was a fearsome sight for opposing pitchers.

since, as people come into the stadium and find their seats, almost invariably their eyes wander to The Spot. Arms point and people stare in admiration. Then they turn to the field and seek out Mantle.

On that same day that he hit the façade Mantle hit a second homer. This one was his 20th of the season and it put him at that date (May 30) 12 games ahead of the pace Babe Ruth followed when he established his quasi-sacred record of 60 in 1927. Other players in other years had excitingly chased Ruth's record. But Mantle, somehow, seemed different from earlier pretenders to Ruth's crown and different, too, from slugging contemporaries like Yogi Berra, whose great skill seems almost methodical, and Dale Long, who is still, despite all, an unknown quantity.

The excitement surrounding Mantle goes beyond numbers, beyond homers hit and homers and games to go. Like Ruth, his violent strength is held in a sheath of powerful, controlled grace. Like Ruth, he makes home run hitting simple and exciting at the same time.

The controlled violence of Mantle's swing produced some of baseball's longest home runs.

The distance he hits his home runs (the approved cliché is "Ruthian blast") takes away the onus of cheapness, a word often applied to the common variety of home run hit today, and leaves the spectator aghast, whether he roots for Mantle or against him.

All this holds true despite the hard fact that heretofore in his five years in the major leagues the most home runs Mantle has hit in one season is 37, whereas Ruth hit 40 or more 11 different times, and two dozen others have hit 40 or more at least once.

Yet where others impress, Mantle awes, and even the knowing professional speaks reverent-

ly of him.... Marty Marion, the unexcitable manager of the Chicago White Sox, described a homer Mantle had hit against the Sox with two out in the ninth to tie a game the Yankees eventually won. "It went way up there," Marty said, with a wry little grin, pointing to the far reaches of the upper stands in deep right-center field. "Way up there. He swung just as easy and *whup!* It was gone. Way up there. I never saw anything like it."

As for the nonprofessional, there is no question that Mantle is the new excitement, the new Ruth. Like Ruth, he is known to those who don't know baseball, magically, the way Ruth

was. A 7-year-old boy, just on the edge of interest in baseball and in bed getting over the measles, watched part of a Yankee game on television. Later he was not quite sure what teams had been playing and he wasn't positive of the score, but when he was asked if he had seen Mickey Mantle bat, his red-speckled face lit up and he said, excitedly, "He hit a big one!"

Of course, Mantle wasn't the only one to hit "big ones" in this year of the slugger. Some said the 1956 version of the lively ball was responsible for the increasingly bullish market in home runs. Others gave credit (or blame) to the growing popularity of the slender-handled willow-wand bat, which bends like a reed when swung hard and breaks easily but which combines concentrated mass and blinding velocity much the way a golf club does. Mantle uses a 32-ounce bat when he hits left-handed, 10 ounces lighter than the bat Ruth used.

Mantle's superb bunting skills and blinding speed made him a multiple threat at the plate.

Whatever the reason, 19 players had hit 10 or more home runs by June 11, an unprecedented number. But Mantle towered above this forest of hitters both for quality and quantity of his home runs. By June 11 only Ruth had hit more home runs up to that point in a season....

Mantle is a switch hitter who knocks the ball well to all fields whether he's batting left-handed or right-handed. More than that, Mantle is a superb bunter and the fastest man in baseball down to first base....

Mantle's greatest problem in his first five years in the majors was a tendency to strike out. This year in spring training he restrained his need to crush the ball with his bat every time he swung, and he struck out only once in the exhibition season. This restraint, applied in the regular season, did not keep his strikeout total quite so dramatically low but it did increase his control of the bat, his ability to meet the ball and, therefore, his domination over the pitcher. Meeting the ball gave him a lot more line-drive base hits and a batting average that has scorched along near or above .400 all season, and his natural strength sent more of those base hits over the outfield barriers than ever before....

Some time, maybe, Mantle will have the curiosity to go back some 29 years, to a day of grandeur such as he may live to enjoy himself. If so, this is what he will read in the *New York Times* of October 1, 1927:

"Babe Ruth scaled the hitherto unattained heights yesterday. Home Run 60, a terrific smash off the southpaw pitching of Zachary, nestled in the Babe's favorite spot in the right field bleachers....

"While the crowd cheered and the Yankee players roared their greetings the Babe made his triumphant, almost regal tour of the paths. He jogged around slowly, touched each bag firmly and carefully, and when he imbedded his spikes in the rubber disk to record officially Homer 60, hats were tossed in the air, papers were torn up and tossed liberally and the spirit of celebration permeated the place....

"The Babe's stroll out to his position was the signal for a handkerchief salute in which all the bleacherites, to the last man, participated..."

"The ball ... was fast, low and inside. The Babe pulled away from the plate, then stepped into the ball and wham! ... it was about 10 feet fair and curving rapidly to the right.

"The ball which became Homer 60 was caught by Joe Forner, of 1937 First Avenue, Manhattan."

Through the jargon of that anonymous writer seeps the unmistakable hallmark of high sporting drama. Whether Mickey himself will ever know a similar moment depends as much on his ability to emulate Ruth's poise and presence and competitive spark as it does on his bat, but his broad, broad back seems ready to receive the mantle of the Babe.

The Prime

1957–1964

Tiger Stadium · 1961

Winning the Triple Crown in 1956
moved Mickey Mantle to the top of the class. For five

years he had shown brilliance, the promise of great things to come. Now he had emerged as the best player in the game. He didn't always remain on that pinnacle, but through most of the next decade he stayed pretty close to it. He won the American League's Most Valuable Player award in 1956, and he won it again in '57 and for a third time in '62. No player has ever won it four times.

He had become the dominant home run hitter in the American League, maybe in the majors. Over the eight seasons from 1955 through '62 no other player in either league hit as many as Mantle did, not in the regular season or in the World Series. He was a tremendously exciting player to watch. It was not just the power of his bat but the emotion he created. As Roy Terrell of *Sports Illustrated* wrote to me after Mantle's death on August 13, 1995, "God bless him. Boy, how he could hit a baseball! And run? But then you know all that." Everyone who saw him play knew all that, the thrill of watching him move, seeing him hit the ball, wondering what he would do next.

by Robert W. Creamer

Baseball's great appeal lies in the combination of anticipation and accomplishment: what might happen and then what *does* happen, either way. Mantle at bat was the epitome of this: the tension as he cocked his bat and the pitcher prepared to throw. He might strike out—an explosive, breath-deflating moment—or he might belt one—to roaring exultation from the stands.

His Yankees won pennants almost every year, and in the World Series Mantle always seemed drenched in drama. He was injured so often at Series time: the bad knee in 1951; a pulled hamstring in '55; a damaged shoulder in '57; a bleeding abscess in his thigh in '61. The image that persists is of the wounded warrior rising to fight again. He rose and fought again so superbly that no one else has hit as many home runs in Series play as Mantle did, nor batted in as many runs, nor scored as many. The World Series was his.

For me, his definitive moment came in the fifth game of the 1956 World Series, a game remembered not for Mantle, but for Don Larsen, who that day pitched his never-to-be-forgotten perfect game. Sal Maglie, Brooklyn's best pitcher down the stretch that season, matched Larsen out for out in the early innings. When Mantle came to bat with two out in the fourth

inning no man on either team had reached base; 23 batters had gone out in succession.

The right-handed Maglie feared Mantle, who was batting lefty, and kept his pitches on the outside edge of the plate to keep Mantle from pulling one into the short right field stands in Yankee Stadium. He had pitched that way to Mantle in the first inning, getting him to hit an easy fly to left field. Now he followed the same strategy. It was a fascinating duel, the deft Maglie trying to paint the outside of the plate, the pull-hitting Mantle refusing to take the bait. Suddenly Maglie came inside, trying to cross up Mantle with a curve in on the hands. But Mantle fisted the ball and lifted a line drive to right field that just cleared the fence inside the foul pole for a stunning home run that put Larsen and the Yankees ahead 1–0, all the scoring Larsen needed, though New York added a run later in the game.

An inning later Mantle raced far back into left-center field, the old Yankee Stadium's "Death Valley," to make a backhanded grab of a line drive while running at top speed away from the plate. Larsen went on to complete his perfect game but Mantle was the man who won it for him and then saved it. Just doing his job.

Mantle looked heavenward (left) as his 49th home run flew out of the park in 1961.

All Hail the Hero Mighty Mickey

by Gerald Holland

With the Triple Crown and a fourth World Series championship in 1956 came a new level of celebrity for Mantle. Once simply a star, he was now that uniquely modern phenomenon, the superstar—part athlete, part corporate entity, part icon. Sports Illustrated's Gerald Holland wrote this memorable profile of Mantle as his celebrity was approaching its peak.

The magic numeral 7 on his back, his right leg bandaged from ankle to thigh, a plastic shield protecting an arrested bone infection called osteomyelitis on his left ankle, the Hero began seriously to condition his great, powerful body this week in the warm, unfailing sunshine of St. Petersburg, Florida.

The Hero was 25 years old and already a legend. By his deeds and by his courageous triumph over his physical handicaps, he was Everybody's dream miraculously come to life. He was being hailed as baseball's alltime superstar. He could do everything: he could run with the speed of a jack rabbit, he could throw strikes to home plate from deep in the outfield: a switch-hitter, he could blast a ball farther than any man who ever lived. He was Elmer the Great, Frank Merriwell and a blond Li'l Abner rolled into one. He was a Walter Mitty vision for every man to see. He was a baseball scout's favorite fantasy in the flesh: a sprig that had been found blooming on a sandlot in the back country, a free agent with no strings on him, a kid to whom $1,100 offered as a bonus for signing looked like all the money in Oklahoma.

That was what the Hero had cost the New York Yankees, the richest baseball club in the world. But if it had been a good deal for the Yankees, it had been a better deal for him. For baseball, as the Hero's dedicated father had meticulously and desperately planned it for his first-born son, had meant emancipation from the relative slavery of the lead mine or the mill. And the Yankees' kind of baseball had meant a great deal more. It had given the Hero a proper arena for his magnificent talents and a proud tradition for him to rise to, the uniform of Ruth

A '53 Series homer brought congrats from Yogi Berra (left), Gil McDougald (15) and Hank Bauer (9).

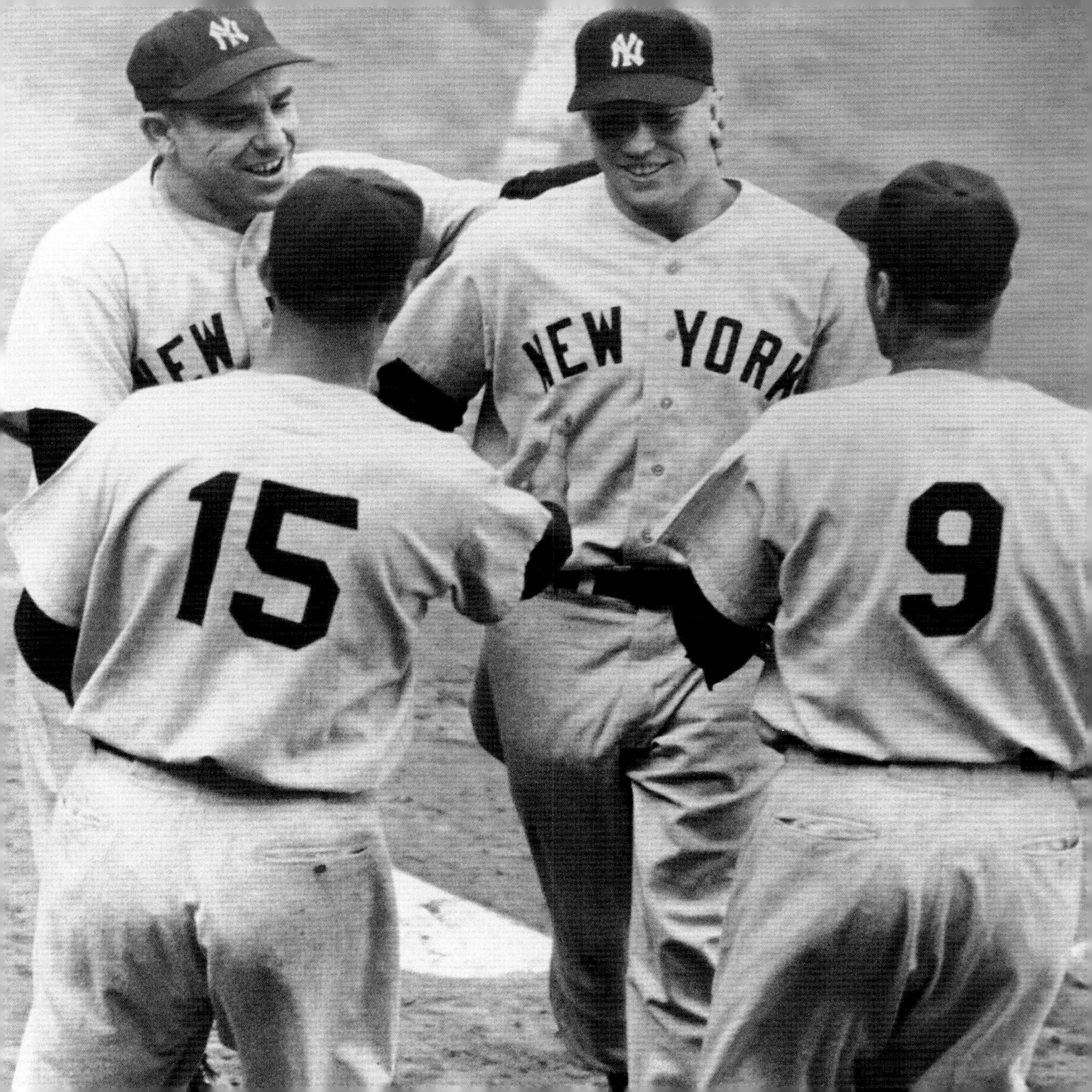
NEW YORK
15
9

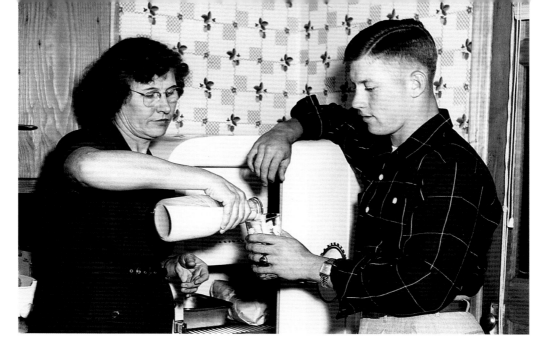

and Gehrig and DiMaggio to inspire him and the incomparable baseball witchery of old Casey Stengel to draw out and to nourish his wondrous native skills.

He had come to these exalted Yankees, at age 19, cast in the role of a Ring Lardner rube. But innately, like his father before him, he was wise with a country boy's wisdom, sharp with small-town perception, keen with a peculiarly middle western brand of gentle wit. He had these qualities when he came to the city but, in his lack of city sophistication, he hid them and, in stark ter-ror of saying something ridiculous, he resorted to the tactic of saying nothing at all. But some-times, when he played badly, he betrayed himself in tantrums for what he was above all else: a boy, a kid traveling incredibly fast and far.

But that was yesterday. The Hero who began spring training in St. Petersburg this week was catching up with himself. Still reticent, still wary of strangers, nevertheless he had come a long, long way along the path that led out of the backyard in Commerce, Oklahoma, where, as toddler, he had swung his first broomstick bat.

In 1951 Mantle and his mother, Lovell, illustrated the Yankee rookie's alleged fondness for milk.

The Hero, Mickey Charles Mantle, had left the country boy far behind. The great center fielder of Yankee Stadium, the Home Run King, the Triple Crown winner and Most Valuable Player of 1956, the recipient of all the awards he cared to hold still for, now was also president of Mickey Mantle Enterprises, president of the Mickey Mantle Motel Corporation, vice-president of the Southwest Chat Company of Baxter Springs, Kansas, dealers in railroad ballast. He drove a brand-new Lincoln. He lived in no ballplayers' hotel for spring training, but in a house out at the beach near St. Petersburg with his wife, Merlyn, and their children, Mickey Jr., four, and David, one. He employed a maid for his wife, who had done all her own housework in the two-bedroom, red-cedar shingle house back in Commerce. In a bedroom closet of the beach house hung the first dinner jacket he has ever owned. In New York, he retained a personal agent to handle his television appearances and endorsement fees and a lawyer to advise him on how to invest an income that could reach $125,000 this year.

The boy who had come to New York at 19 and promptly signed away 50% of his outside income (it amounted to $45,000 in 1956) to a perfect stranger (a matter still in the law courts) now was well protected against exploitation. He had a great and good friend and adviser in Harold D. Youngman of Baxter Springs, Kansas, the builder of super-highways who put Mickey on the payroll at $500 a month when, as a Yankee rookie, he needed an off-season job. In Tom Greenwade, the Yankee scout who signed him, he had a paternal counselor from his own part of the country who spoke his language and talked as straight to him as the father who had died at 39. In Billy Martin, his roommate on the road, and Whitey Ford, the pitching star, he had pals who knew where the laughs were.

And yet, Mickey stood a little apart from them all. For, as he had learned along a sometimes torturous winter banquet circuit, he was now public property. Because of television, more people had seen him play than had seen Babe Ruth in his entire career; Mickey had unique responsibilities, and the banquet speakers did not hesitate to remind him of what they were. As they flattered him and extolled him, they also admonished him and instructed him and rebuked him. They called upon him to live every public and private moment in a manner that would dismay a saint. "We fathers can do only so much, Mickey," said one speaker, forgetting that Mickey is a father, too. "It is up to you to set the example for our kids." Other orators told him to watch his language, to curb his temper, to hold his head up after striking out, to eschew bad balls, to forgo so much as a kick at the dugout water cooler in anger—and to hit at least 61 home runs in 1957. Men clutching microphones called upon Mickey for a display of virtue to which few men dare aspire themselves. And a Broadway press agent, a man accustomed to the raw realities of life and sports, privately expressed off-mike horror at what he judged to be one of Mickey's falls from grace. What had Mickey done? He had inquired as to the cash value (about $10,000) of the Hickok Belt which he was awarded at a banquet in Rochester.

Like it or not, Mickey Mantle was stuck with the Hero's role. And this is a report on how he is taking it, written out of a long journey and many hours spent in the company of Mickey and the friends who know him best.

• • •

"To understand Mickey," said Tom [Greenwade, the lean, rawboned Yankee scout who is a part-time Missouri farmer and town school board president], "you have to understand a little about his father Elven, or Mutt, as they called him. Now Mutt loved baseball, but he was no baseball nut. He wanted the best for his boy and he saw baseball as the best way to get it for him. Mutt had a lot of good, common sense and Mickey has, too.

"When Mickey made good with the Yanks, people down here in Oklahoma would come to his father and say, 'Those Yankees stole your boy!' Mutt would shake his head and say, 'No, I don't look at it that way at all. I consider Mick-ey was mighty lucky to get with the Yankees and if I had to advise him all over again, I'd tell him to do just what he did.'"

Tom Greenwade rubbed his chin and shook his head.

"I must admit Mickey himself has needled me more than once about that $1,100 bonus, but Mutt never mentioned it to me at all. Mutt was certainly a rare specimen. He never bothered the ball club or the managers, demanding this or that for his boy. Not that he didn't take the interest. Why, he saw every game when Mickey was at Joplin. He'd work all day in the mines and then drive the 20 miles or more over from Commerce. But he'd never interfere. The strongest words I ever heard from him on the subject of Mickey's progress was after Mickey had had a bad night in the field at Joplin. Mutt said to me, 'Tom, are the Yankees set on that boy as a shortstop?' I said, 'We've been thinking that way, yes.' Mutt nodded his head and then, after a minute, he said, 'You know, I wouldn't be surprised to see Mickey end up in the outfield. He gets a pretty good jump on a fly ball.'"

Tom took a cigarette and a light.

"Here's something about Mickey. Try to push him and he can be stubborn as a mule...."

[A few days later,] I sat in the paneled office of Harold D. Youngman in Baxter Springs, Kansas, a town just a few miles away from

Mantle and Merlyn, with Mickey Jr. (left) and David: The Hero had his own kids to worry about.

Mickey's home in Commerce, Oklahoma. It was in Baxter Springs that Mickey, playing with a local team called the Whiz Kids, first attracted the attention of the New York Yankees....

[Mickey] was wearing a tooth-pick, a suede jacket and a fur cap that had been dyed a bright green and had some kind of insignia on it. I told him he had certainly made a fine speech in Milwaukee.

He turned to Youngman.

"Spoke about 15 minutes," he said, taking the insurance papers Youngman held out to him.... As we walked out, I took another look at Mickey's green fur cap and remarked:

"Is there anything special about that fur cap, Mickey?"

"Nope," said Mickey.

We passed a man in the hall.

"Hi, Mick," he said. "That's one hell of a snazzy cap."

"Yep," said Mickey. "The jet pilots gave it to me when I was up in Alaska with Bob Hope...."

I thought back to what Tom Greenwade had said and what had just happened in Youngman's office. Then it became clear to me. You don't ask an Oklahoma man like Mickey nosy questions about his fur cap. What you do is tell him it's a snazzy cap and then, if there's anything special about it, he'll tell you.....

Billy Martin said of Mickey, "People don't realize the pressures that guy is under. He was the biggest star in the game at 24 and it's not easy to get used to suddenly finding that you can't even sit down and eat a sandwich without being surrounded. They say it's the price of fame and he's getting well paid for it. But still, coming out of a small town in Oklahoma, it takes a little time to learn. Mickey's learned fast and he's grown up fast. Another thing people are apt to forget is that he plays ball under some tough physical handicaps. And he never complains or mentions it. You ask Casey...."

"There was a boy on a quiz program," said Casey. " 'What do you want to be when you grow up?' they ask him. 'Center fielder on the New York Yankees,' the boy says. That's the way it goes. They know him everywhere now. But here's what people don't realize. The big thing about this boy is he likes to play baseball. The knee bothers him and still he comes to me and says, 'Let me play.' Sometimes I let him when I shouldn't. I shouldn't have let him play in the All-Star game. But he says, 'You got to let me play, Casey.' So I give in. I'm wrong, but I let him play. That's what people don't know. With all the other things, dancing on the television and making speeches and going for the records, there's this big thing about this boy. This boy loves to play baseball."

A round of golf with Martin (left) was one of Mantle's earliest methods of relaxation.

From SI: September 30, 1957

Yanks vs. Braves

by Robert W. Creamer

As the baseball fans eagerly looked forward to a World Series matchup that at last featured a team that did not *hail from the Eastern Seaboard—seven of the previous eight had been all-East affairs—Sports Illustrated's Robert W. Creamer mused on the potential delight of watching Milwaukee's Warren Spahn do battle with Mantle. For the record, the Braves took the Series in seven games as Spahn was outshone by teammate Lew Burdette, who pitched three complete-game victories and allowed just two earned runs in 27 innings.*

It is possible that history will not care particularly that this year's World Series will be the first one to be played in the Central Time Zone since 1946. Even the world of baseball, which treasures an infinite variety of strange records, ... neglects to list "Most Consecutive World Series Played East of Toledo, Ohio...."

In ten years, during which 59 separate and reasonably distinct World Series games were played, 54 were played in the East. Worse (this is being slanted for Midwesterners), 49 of the

Mantle led the Yankees into the World Series for the sixth time in his seven big-league seasons.

54 were played in New York City. The World Series, the greatest sports event on the American scene, greater than the New Year's Day bowl games, greater than the Kentucky Derby, greater than the National Open, had deteriorated into just one more Sight to See in New York, ranking well ahead of Grant's Tomb but slightly behind the Empire State Building.

And now, all of a sudden, that era ended. The New York Yankees still have a bulldog grip on the American League's share of the Series, but New York the city has relinquished its monopoly. When you get right down to it, the most appealing thing about the 1957 Series is the fact that the Brooklyn Dodgers aren't in it. This is said with full and appreciative realization that the Brooklyn team now quietly shriveling on the vine of age has been for 10 years one of the truly great baseball teams of all time....

Now, when Mickey Mantle swings his bat in the on-deck circle waiting his turn in the first inning of the third game of the 1957 Series, he will do it in County Stadium in Milwaukee instead of Ebbets Field. Now it will be another setting for the old, old fascination attending battles of champions: how will the Hero do against the New Challenger?

Of course, the most potent arm of the New Challenger belongs to one Warren Spahn, who won 20 games in the major leagues the summer that Mickey Mantle was a 15-year-old kid playing sandlot ball in the Ozark country. Neverthe-

less, Spahn at 36 has played in only one World Series while Mantle at 25 is entering his sixth. Mickey has proved himself in the Series competition; Warren will be on trial. Mickey will bat right-handed against Warren (who is the only left-hander on the Braves' pitching staff, except for part-time workmen Juan Pizarro and Taylor Phillips), and students of the game, who are as fascinated by the individual components of the drama as they are by the whole, will watch this duel between the powerful young hitter and the shrewd old pitcher intently.

That Mantle and Spahn should be symbolic of Yankees and Braves is a singular compliment to each, because each has as teammates some of the most remarkable ballplayers in the major leagues. Mantle has Yogi Berra; Spahn has Henry Aaron. Mantle has Gil McDougald; Spahn the incomparable Red Schoendienst. But Mantle *is* the New York Yankees, the home-run hitter, the powerful slugger, the one player all kids know about, and all old men. And Spahn is the Milwaukee Braves, after years of trying finally making it, the highly skilled artisan now called to the middle of the stage for the crucial test. How Mantle and Spahn do against one another may be symbolic, too, of the way the Series turns.

The odds will undoubtedly favor the Yankees and, by extension, Mantle. This reflects a widespread and rather unjustified lack of confidence in Milwaukee, as well as a time-honored faith in the Yankees.

From SI: June 15, 1959

Mickey the Booster Shot

by Roy Terrell

After losing to the Braves in the 1957 World Series, New York won the rematch in '58, bouncing back from a 3–1 deficit to take the Series in seven games. But the Yankees seemed curiously flat at the start of the '59 season, winning just 12 of their first 32 games. Then, as reported by Sports Illustrated's Roy Terrell, a single swing from the mighty Mantle seemed to turn it all around.

On the afternoon of May 23, in the first inning of a baseball game at Memorial Stadium in Baltimore, a young man in the neat gray road uniform of the New York Yankees walked to the plate, smoothed out the dirt with his spikes and looked at the pitcher. He straightened his batting helmet and wiped his right hand on his hip. He leaned forward in a crouch which seemed to broaden the already incredibly broad back and swung the long, slender bat back and forth in vicious little arcs. The muscles of his forearms rippled and bunched as he tightened his grip.

The Yankees were in trouble. They had won only 12 of their first 32 games, and for the first time in 19 seasons they had tumbled in an undignified heap into the American League cellar. From the most feared team in all baseball the Yankees had become everyone's patsy, losing because they couldn't hit, losing because they couldn't field, losing because their pitching was bad, losing because the rest of the league feared them not.

Then Milt Pappas, the Baltimore pitcher, threw to the plate, Mickey Mantle swung his bat and suddenly the Yankees' troubles were no more.

Mantle doubled to drive in a run. Later that afternoon he walked. He walked again. He hit a home run and a single. He stole third base and went on in to score when the catcher's throw was wide. He scored two other runs. The Yankees won 13–5....

In 15 games since that Saturday afternoon in Baltimore, Mantle had batted .412, scored 17 runs, driven in 13, walked 16 times, stolen six bases and hit four home runs. And the Yankees had won 11 of those 15 games to come roaring up out of the cellar. By the time they had finished with Cleveland last weekend, winning

When Mantle began connecting again, the struggling Yankees emerged from their slump.

three games out of four from a team that had spent all but five days of the season in first place, the Yankees were sixth, but only 3½ games behind, and the rest of the American League was running for the hills.

Of course, other people besides Mantle helped the Yankee surge. Turley, Ford, Larsen and Ditmar pitched exceptionally well. McDougald snapped out of his slump, and Hector Lopez, brought in from the Athletics in a trade, drove in runs at a terrific rate. But the Yankees themselves admitted that the spark had come from Mantle.

"There's no question about it," said McDougald. "The way he's playing has lifted the whole team...."

"You might say," said Stengel, "that he is making full use of his abilities, and therefore is playing better than anyone in this league for a long time."

As Stengel so often says, the things Mantle can do are "amazing." But to millions of baseball fans, especially those right in his own home park, the most amazing thing about Mickey Mantle is why he doesn't do them all the time.

No one ever looked more like a great athlete. Mantle is just under six feet tall and, in top condition, weighs 195 pounds. His legs are trim and powerful. His torso is like that of a weight lifter, thick and muscular, and his shoulders are very broad. His arms are big and bulge with knots of hard muscle. And from the 18-inch neck rises a good-looking blond head and an almost handsome face in a slightly tough, slightly insolent, American-boy sort of way, with its uptilted nose and widespread eyes....

His speed, of course, is legend and, again as Stengel says, "nobody that big ever ran so fast." His power is legend, too: the home run he hit in Washington in 1953 practically invented the tape measure: only Mantle and Williams have ever hit a baseball over the roof in Detroit; only Mantle ever hit a ball up so high against the façade in right field at Yankee Stadium. He hits home runs left-handed and he hits them right-handed—which of course no one else has ever done with any consistency before—and one year he hit 52 of them.

In 1956 he led the American League—in fact, all of baseball—in batting and home runs and runs batted in. Another time he hit .365, but won no championship because Ted Williams hit even higher. Twice, before his 26th birthday, he was named the Most Valuable Player in the league. He has had some great years, and he is only 27 now.

He has also had some bad years, particularly when you consider how good Mickey Mantle might be. Only twice has he driven in more than 100 runs, and his lifetime average after

43

Mantle in his prime was that rare combination of awesome power and lightning speed.

44

human being. He is not a very complex human being, but he is still a human being and therefore complicated enough. He came up to the Yankees at the age of 19 from the farm and mining country of Oklahoma, a man physically but a shy, scared boy inside, dressed in an ill-fitting $8 suit. He had been raised to be a ballplayer and that was all that he knew....

Today Mantle is no longer scared, although even with those he knows he remains shy until he knows them very well. He is a very wealthy young man, with one of baseball's biggest salaries and two profitable outside business interests. He dresses well in beautifully cut suits, drives a big car, eats at the best places, plays golf at the best clubs....

His appetites have increased with fame and financial security, and today this is the criticism one hears most often. On Babe Ruth, who hit 60 home runs, living it up looked good. On Mickey Mantle, who may never hit 50 again, it brings bushels of dark, disapproving frowns. If, they say, this kid, with all his great talent, would devote himself to baseball, if he would live and think baseball and take care of himself, he could become the greatest player who ever lived. Maybe so. Certainly Mantle agrees, at least down on the field, for no one ever tried harder to excel or suffered more when he failed. But somewhere along the way, when the big

eight seasons and despite the two great ones is only .316. For the normal big leaguer, even for the very good one these days, this would be superb. But not for a Mantle.

Much of the trouble, of course, is due to injuries. He has been hurt often, particularly in the legs, and frequently these have been injuries which would put others on the bench. "He never played a game for me," says Stengel, "that he wasn't all taped up. I ask him how he feels and he says, 'O.K.' I ask him if he wants to play and he says, 'I want to play.' So I need him and I let him play. What should I do? Tie him to the bench?"

There is also the matter of Mantle, the

Mantle (right) robbed Larry Doby in '57, the kind of play Stengel (above) called "amazing."

decision came up—whether or not to live like a Trappist monk and supplant Ruth and Cobb in the record books and earn $200,000 a year— Mickey decided to enjoy life and earn only $80,000 a year and be content with being merely the most colorful and exciting and best ballplayer in his league during his own time.

So while the adulation he receives now is greater than ever before, so are the boos....

Whether it is too late now for the miracle to occur, no one really knows. He has been stealing bases as never before, but even Stengel admits that this was simply because the team was not hitting and they had to get some runs some way. ...

Mantle has been hitting well despite the fact that pitchers seldom give him anything good to work on and despite his injuries. He wraps his right knee before every game, and his right shoulder, which he hurt in a collision with Red Schoendienst in the 1957 World Series, still troubles him when he swings left-handed very hard. Worse, it hurts when he raises his arm above a certain height, and this has forced him to make some small but bothersome alterations in his stance.

If Mantle continues to hit, the Yankees will probably win the pennant again, especially if he continues to play the way he did during his two-week reign of terror. He may never make anyone forget Ruth or Cobb, but he is a whale of a ballplayer nevertheless. As McDougald says, the kind who can carry a team.

From SI: July 4, 1960

Double M for Murder

by Walter Bingham

Though Mantle's bat lifted the Yankees out of the cellar in May 1959, the season proved to be a disappointment nonetheless as New York's proud dynasty finished the season at a very mortal 79–75, a dismal 15 games behind the pennant-winning Chicago White Sox. As the '60 season opened, many observers were openly wondering whether the Yankees' glory days were all in the past. But a new player named Roger Maris arrived that season and soon the Yanks were back on top. Sports Illustrated's Walter Bingham wrote one of the first stories on what would soon become one of baseball's most productive pairings: Mantle and Maris.

Someday people may talk of the Great Yankee Slump, that brief period in the history of the American League when the mice whipped the cat. It began, they may remember, on August 9, 1958 when the New York Yankees, leading the league by 16½ games, lost a game to the Boston Red Sox 9–6. It ended on June 7, 1960 when the Yankees defeated the Chicago White Sox 5–2. They beat the White Sox again the next day and the next, then won two games from Cleveland, two from Kansas City and four more from Chicago. Last week they continued to win—two games from Detroit, two from Cleveland. The Yankees had won 15 out of 19 games and were in first place. The Great Slump was over, the cat was on the prowl, and the mice of the league were looking for a place to hide.

That period between August of 1958 and June of 1960 was one of almost continuous pain for the Yankees. They lost 25 of their last 44 games in 1958, and although they won the pennant, their fourth in a row, and the World Series, they were sick and they knew it. The spring of 1959 brought no improvement. The Yankees fell to last place in May and eventually finished a poor third with a record of 79 games won, 75 games lost. This season the Yankees lost 20 of their first 41 games—making 120 losses in 239 games—and they floundered in fourth place. And then, without warning, they snapped out of it.

There are many reasons for the Yankee resurgence. "Tell them we started winning when the old man got back," said one player sarcastically

Mantle at the plate and Maris in the on deck circle spelled trouble for opposing pitchers.

(a majority of the Yankee players dislike Casey Stengel). Nonetheless, it is true that the team started winning the day Stengel returned after a week's illness.

A more concrete reason is the powerful and timely hitting of Mickey Mantle. "When he hits we move," said pitcher Art Ditmar. Mantle, in the worst slump of his up-and-down career in April and May, cracked out of it in early June. During the three weeks of the Yankee rampage Mantle hit well over .400, with 18 runs batted in and eight home runs....

Then there is Hector Lopez, who has been hitting well in the No. 2 spot, just in front of Mantle.... But, good as Mantle and Lopez have been lately, it is extremely doubtful that the Yankees would be in first place were it not for their new right fielder, Roger Maris....

[Maris] gives some credit for his fast start this season to the good-hitting Yankees who surround him in the batting order—Mantle before him, [Moose] Skowron (before he was hurt), [Yogi] Berra or [Elston] Howard after him.... Batting directly after Mantle does present one problem, however. In December, Mantle hit a home run off Frank Lary. When Maris got up, the first pitch was way inside, forcing him back from the plate. A few innings later Mantle hit another home run off Lary. This time the first pitch to Maris was directly over the top of his head.... (Mantle, incidentally, is also frequently thrown at, but with him it is his legs. Knowing Mantle has a bad right knee, it is standard procedure with American League pitchers to make him skip rope periodically....)

As Maris and Mantle devastated the western teams with their hitting, the press began to link the two names in the tradition of Ruth and Gehrig. "The buzz-saw team," one Detroit writer called them. "Double M for Murder," said another. Mel Allen, reaching, called them "the gold dust twins" on one occasion and "those magical marvels, Mantle and Maris," on another. Casey Stengel provided the most succinct description. "The fella in right does the job if the other fella doesn't," Casey said....

Ditmar, who after a slow start won four straight games, praises the hitting. "I'm pitching the same as I did earlier in the season, but now I'm getting runs."

A few hours later Ditmar was on the mound, trying to hold on to a 3–2 lead. He got out of the seventh inning, but he was tired and the Tigers were closing in. Then, leading off the Yankee eighth, Lopez tripled, Mantle doubled and Maris, on a 3–0 pitch, hit a towering home run. With three swings the Yankees had wrapped up another game. It was just like old times, and the Yankees looked like the Damn Yankees again.

49

With Maris providing him powerful support in the lineup, Mantle was able to relax a bit more.

From SI: April 17, 1961

Yes, There *Is* a New Mantle

by Tex Maule

As the 1961 season opened, Mantle was ready to assume the leadership of the Yankees. As reported by Sports Illustrated's Tex Maule, he was healthy, relaxed, more mature—primed to have his best season since his triple crown triumph five years earlier. The final '61 stats made Maule appear prescient: 54 home runs, 128 RBIs and a .317 batting average, as predicted Mantle's best season since '56.

Ralph Houk, manager of the New York Yankees, moved in a small circle in the team dressing room, eying an imaginary pop fly. A small group of players, in various stages of undress, watched him. One clutched his stomach with both arms and doubled over with helpless laughter even before Houk finished his story. He was Mickey Mantle.

"Finally, the ball came down and he missed it by five feet," Houk said, making a desperate lunge for the ball. "Then he looked at it lying on the ground and started to sneak up on it." Houk eyed a patch of bare floor and stalked it in elaborate pantomime. All the players were laughing now, Mantle rocking back and forth with glee.

"Finally, he pounced on the ball and dug a hole and buried it, right there behind home plate," Houk said, suiting action to his words.

"Holy gee," said Mantle, between gasps of laughter. "Holy gee."

He finished suiting up slowly, listening to Yogi Berra tell about a trip he took to Venezuela during which an irate fan tried to pink a manager with a .45 for taking out a pitcher. Again Mantle doubled up with laughter.

He wrapped his left leg in a long rubber bandage, extending from below the calf to above his weak knee. Earlier he had had heat treatment for his right shoulder and supersonic treatment for pulled stomach muscles. But he was cheerful, relaxed and happy when he walked out of the dressing room into the bright morning sunshine at Miller Huggins Field in St. Petersburg.

One of the ubiquitous photographers who dog the Yankees watched Mantle and shook his head unbelievingly. "He waved and hollered hello at me in the parking lot a little while ago," he said. "What's happened to him?..."

On the field, in the dugout or at the plate—wherever you looked there was a new, looser Mantle.

This is the new Mickey Mantle—relaxed, confident, easily moved to laughter, quick to forget affront, approachable. He had his best spring since 1956 (the year he hit 52 home runs), hitting the ball with violence from both sides of the plate, fielding with his usual casual grace and effectiveness. Early on, Houk had said that this is the year Mantle takes over as the Yankee team leader; unconsciously, Mantle has done so. In the bull sessions in the dressing room the stories are directed to Mantle, his opinion is asked.

"I don't know about the leader thing," Mantle said one morning. "It depends on how I do. You hit .350, you're a leader. You hit .250, you're not. These guys are pros. They don't want a .250 leader. Nobody does."

He sat before his locker, wearing only the knee-length shorts the Yankees wear under their uniforms. He is a blocky man, maybe 20 pounds heavier now, after 10 years, than he was as a 19-year-old rookie. His face was serious: he is not an introspective man and he was thinking, now, of how he had changed in 10 years.

"I guess in the last year or so I've learned how to take the bad days," he said slowly. "You know, the days you go 0 for 4. I can forget them now. Used to be I'd worry."

He was quiet again for a moment.

"I didn't make up my mind to forget them," he said. "It wasn't anything like that. It just came on gradually. Funny thing, if I go 0 for 4 and we lose, the writers make a big thing out of me not hitting. Somebody else, who may be hitting for a better average, goes 0 for 4, and they don't notice it."

He grinned suddenly.

"Works the other way, too," he said. "I get a single and drive in a run and we win a ball game and they pay more attention to that than to a home run by somebody else. Billy Martin used to kid me about that. We had a lot of fun together. One year we hit home runs in the same game about eight times. Billy would read me the story and it would tell about my home run, how long it was, you know. Then at the end he'd say, 'P.S. Martin also homered....' "

He was ready to leave now, but he waited a moment. "You have all you need?" he asked courteously. "If you want anything else, holler."

He walked away, a compact, wide figure in sport shirt and slacks, surprisingly small. Ralph Houk, who had finished dressing by now, too, watched him go.

"[Mantle]'s grown up," Houk said. "He's a man now. Mature. I think his mind's at ease and it shows in the way he plays. He's happy about the money he's getting and that makes a difference, too.... He's in better shape this year than he has been during the spring for a long time...."

"He's got great potential," he said. "He could have another year like 1956. I hope he does."

Mantle's '61 season of dreams produced 54 homers, the last one coming on this shot against Boston.

From SI: July 31, 1961

Assault on the Record

by Walter Bingham

By late July 1961 the speculation had become intense. Who would win the home run race, Mantle or Maris? And would either of them be able to match Ruth's seemingly unassailable mark of 60 home runs in a single season? Sports Illustrated's Walter Bingham offered his thoughts on the subject and on the national hysteria surrounding the pursuit of the Babe.

Of all the records in sports, none is more honored, none more renowned than the 60 home runs Babe Ruth hit in 1927. Since then many men have seriously attacked it, but for every June challenge there has been a September reckoning. Twice men have come close. Jimmy Foxx and Hank Greenberg each hit 58 home runs, Foxx in 1932, Greenberg six years later. No one has done that well since, but last week, as the season moved into its second half, it began to look as if Ruth's record finally might fall. The challenge comes not from one man but two, Mickey Mantle and Roger Maris, teammates on the New York Yankees.

Mantle and Maris, with 37 and 36 home runs apiece, are currently running about 20 games ahead of the pace Ruth set in 1927. Mantle hit his 37th home run in the Yankees' 92nd game, Ruth did not hit his 37th until the Yankees' 114th game. Such comparisons with Ruth's pace have always been deceptive, however, since Ruth hit so many of his home runs late in the season. After 123 games of the 1927 season, Ruth had hit only 40 home runs, but in his last 32 games he hit 20, 17 of them in September. (Ruth's late surge crushed his teammate, Lou Gehrig, who was tied with Ruth 44–44 on Labor Day. Gehrig finished with 47.) Any serious challenger must go into September with a cushion.

Mantle hit his first home run this season in the Yankees' third game, and he quickly opened up an 8–1 lead over Maris, who didn't hit *his* first until the Yankees' 11th game. But in May Maris reduced the lead to 14–12, and in June he passed Mantle by hitting 15 home runs. Maris led Mantle by four at the All-Star break, but then Mantle rallied to take the lead. In a game at Boston last week Maris hit a home run to tie Mantle, who touched his teammate's hand in

Rarely this chummy, Maris (right) and Mantle nonetheless goaded one another to new heights.

salute and then hit a home run to regain his lead. This competition between the two, even if friendly, should be beneficial to both players. Just as Roger Bannister needed Chris Chataway to help him break the four-minute mile, Maris and Mantle are an ever-present stimulus to each other....

The duel between the two Yankee sluggers has drawn capacity crowds during the team's latest road trip. In Chicago, Baltimore (where both players lost home runs in a rained-out game), Washington and Boston, the cheers for Mantle and Maris matched those usually reserved for the home-town heroes. The New York newspapers have devoted their blackest print to the home run battle, MICK 37, ROG 36 one headline read last week. When Tony Kubek hit a single to drive home the winning run in extra innings, a headline reported YANKS WIN, MARIS (35) SAVES GAME....

In the midst of all this excitement, Ford Frick, the commissioner of baseball, last week made a formal statement on the subject. Because the American League is playing a 162-game schedule this season, he said, Babe Ruth's record would not be considered broken if a player hit the decisive home runs after his club's 154th game. It was a foolish, pathetic little statement, foolish because it makes so little sense, pathetic because it will be ignored.

It was Frick himself who sanctioned the American League's 162-game schedule, and if he had a statement to make regarding records that might be broken because of the additional games, he should have made it before the season began. Just why Frick picked 154 games is puzzling, too. It is true that the old schedule called for that number of games, but the Yankees of 1927 played 155 games, since one game ended in a tie....

To make Mantle and Maris do in part of a season what Ruth did in an entire season is clearly unfair. A season is a season, no matter how many games are played, and if Mantle hits 61 home runs this year, the answer to the question of who has hit the most home runs in one season will be Mickey Mantle. Besides, no crowd watching Mantle's 61st home run sailing out of the park will be talked out of the conviction that it has just seen a new record being set....

What Ruth was to baseball in his generation no man can ever hope to duplicate. He needs no legislation to be remembered and honored, and this is the most unfortunate and unforgivable aspect of Ford Frick's decision. Frick's attempt to protect the record, undoubtedly well-intentioned, is an insult to the man who set it. Ruth was always a man to accept a challenge. He probably would be happy to spot Mantle and Maris a few extra games.

Mantle's three homers in the '60 Series against Pittsburgh were a sign of things to come in '61.

From SI: April 2, 1962

Mantle and Maris in the Movies

by Robert W. Creamer

In the aftermath of the '61 season, Maris, the new home-run king, and Mantle, the hero who battled through injury to stay with Maris step-for-step until September, were in demand everywhere. Numerous offers were rejected, but when Hollywood called, Mantle and Maris answered, agreeing to appear in a film called Safe at Home!, *in the seemingly simple roles of themselves. As reported by Sports Illustrated's Robert W. Creamer, the job proved to be tougher than a scorching doubleheader in mid-August.*

There's this little kid, see, and he's crazy about Mickey Mantle and Roger Maris. He and his father—his mother is dead—live on this boat in Florida. But they used to live in New York, and so one day in the Little League the kid boasts that he knows Mantle and Maris, and he says that he'll get them to come to the Little League banquet they're about to have. Now he's in the soup, because he's lying, see? He really doesn't know Mantle and Maris at all. So the kid runs away and goes down to the New York Yankees' spring training camp in Fort Lauderdale and he manages to meet Mantle and Maris and he explains what happened and he asks them to get him off the hook. But they tell him, no, they won't come to the banquet because he has told a lie. So then the kid goes back home and bravely admits that he lied, and then Roger and Mickey invite the whole damn Little League down to Lauderdale to watch spring training and everything comes out O.K. Oh, it ought to make a hell of a picture, a real grabber.

Safe at Home!, starring Mickey Mantle and Roger Maris, is a Naud-Hamilburg production (their first), a Columbia Pictures Corp. release (their 1,706th), a classic B picture; it was designed for cheap, quick filming, an April release date and a fast buck. It is not quite the same sort of thing as *Twist Around the Clock*, which is known in the trade as *Son of Rock Around the Clock*. It is in a grander tradition, in the hereditary line of epics like Babe Ruth in *The Babe Comes Home*, Lou Gehrig in *Rawhide*, Jack Dempsey in *Manhattan Madness*. True, the plot has a familiar ring: kid gets in trouble, kid runs away, kid is befriended by gruff but

Makeup session: Despite some heckling from teammates, Mantle was startlingly professional.

kindly hero who solves his problem, kid ends up smiling with happiness.... Still, it *is* different. There are two gruff but kindly heroes instead of one—three, if you count William Frawley, who plays a Yankee coach—and the trouble the boy gets into is in the contemporary, downbeat mode—it's all in his mind.

Essentially, the movie is like all movies starring nonacting celebrities: it's a guest appearance, designed to draw the crowds while the celebrity is still of red-hot interest to the public. Tom Naud, the dark-visaged, good-looking, 35-year-old producer of the film, says the idea came to him last summer. "Every headline you saw said M & M," he said in Fort Lauderdale a few weeks ago during the filming of the picture. "You couldn't buy that kind of publicity for a million dollars...."

Of course it wasn't ... easy. Nobody works harder than movie people, despite the hallowed myth that they lead lives of hedonistic luxury and comfort. Every morning during the 10 days of shooting in Fort Lauderdale the movie troupe was up at 6, out of the motel at 7 and on location well before 8, and so were Mantle and Maris on the days they were needed. Much of the film has an outdoor locale ... and so shooting went on all day long each day, with a half-hour break for lunch, until sundown. And then, on several occasions, they went on working far into the evening, doing the various night sequences....

Mantle and Maris, who had been remarkably calm and patient most of the time—as visions of dollars danced in their heads—got just a little tired, too. They took with good-natured grins the broad humor of their confreres in the locker room as they were being made up ("How you like my suntan?" Mantle asked late arrival Bill Stafford), and most of the time on the field they were fine with the Little Leaguers, who had been instructed to inundate the two players with questions. Like all Little Leaguers en masse, they were loud, persistent, repetitive and impossible ("Do you think you're as good as Ted Williams?" "Who's the best player in the league?" "How come you hit 61 home runs?" "Why didn't *you* hit 61 home runs?" "Do the Yankees own their own airplane?"). It got to be nerve-racking because there was no end to it. After each take, when the others—[manager Ralph] Houk, for example—could relax for a minute or two, the kids stayed glued to Mantle and Maris, stepping on their feet, pulling their sleeves, firing questions. The kids hardly seemed to notice when they were on camera and when they were not. Earlier, when they had first arrived at the ball park and had been brought into the locker room to meet Mantle and Maris, they had been subdued and polite and, when they were called out onto the field again, had filed past the players as though they were on a receiving line. One kid said, "Goodbye, Mr. Maris," and another, furtively touching Roger's biceps as he passed, said quietly, "Wow." But outside they were loud and

aggressive, and after an hour of it Mantle finally complained with some anger to an assistant director: "How long do we got to stand here?" Later, in a corner of the field, alone with Maris, he said wonderingly, "I never saw such a business. Seems you stand around all day doing nothing and then do about five minutes of the show...."

For the beginning of the final sequence—for long shots—the kids were piled back into the tunneled runway under the stands that leads from the locker room to the dugout. On cue they were to pile out of the tunnel, race up the dugout steps, charge across the field and surround Mantle and Maris, yelling all the way. They rehearsed it two or three times, which was something to see, the kids roaring out and racing, yelling, across the grass. "Fellows, take it easy," cried an assistant director. "We don't want to know who's the fastest boy." The effort of getting the Little Leaguers back into the tunnel after each repeat was a tremendous one, like forcing 50 blown-up balloons back into the

For the most part Mantle and Maris handled the press of Little Leaguers with admirable grace.

box they came in. "Back, boys! Back! Back up, now! Boys! Back up there!" "Hit 'em with a bat," a member of the camera crew suggested. "Boys," finally spoke [Walter] Doniger, the director, a soft-voiced man who seemed the antithesis of the tyrant the director is traditionally supposed to be. "Now, boys," he said like a teacher, "when I talk you have to listen to me." They listened, sort of, and slowly retreated into the tunnel.

"O.K., now," said the first assistant director. "Quiet behind the camera."

"All right, Howard."

"Here we go, Burt."

"Roll 'em."

"Action!"

Out of the tunnel the boys poured, and up the steps of the dugout. Bryan Russell, the 9-year-old actor who plays [the boy] Hutch, led the mob, but he tripped on the top step of the dugout and fell flat on his face.

"Cut," ordered Doniger dejectedly, and everything stopped—except the Little Leaguers, who

Frawley (right), of *I Love Lucy* fame, joked with Houk during one of the interminable breaks.

roared past the fallen Bryan and continued their wild charge towards Mantle and Maris.

"Hold it!" yelled Doniger. "*Hold it!*" And he and an assistant director, trying to save time, raced out in front of the horde waving their hands, trying to stem the tide, yelling "Hold it, hold it," slowing and finally stopping the boys.

Behind them, Mantle spoke. "One got through," he pointed out cheerfully.

Another bit had the boys leaving the athletes and running out onto the playing field. They disappeared from camera range as they crossed the baselines but, baseball players all, they kept right on running until they got to their positions, including distant left, center and right fields. Tongues began to hang after two rehearsals, since the boys—with the exception of the three who were professional actors—ran back in at full speed, too. Doniger spoke to them. "Fellows," he said, "don't run all the way out. Just run out past the baseline. Stop right out there in the middle, near the—uh, uh—near the—uh...."

"The pitcher's mound," Mantle helped out.

Doniger smiled. "I would have figured that one out myself, Mickey."

Mantle, smiling, cocked a glance at Tom Naud.

"Honest, Mick," Naud said. "Wally knows where first base is...."

Right through the last day of shooting, when Maris and Mantle and Frawley and the boy were playing interior scenes, the two top players remained startlingly professional and serious, except for their moans about the delays. There was almost no horseplay on the set, and few wisecracks—except from Frawley. When the makeup man would move in quickly, in an interval between takes, to fix Mantle's makeup or mop some sweat from Maris' forehead, they submitted quietly, with no resentment or embarrassment. When a sportswriter called Mickey "Marlon Mantle," Mickey smiled as though it were a good joke but a pretty old one. When Maris blew a line he walked away from the camera a few feet muttering in disgust, as though he'd just got a bad call at home plate, but there was only irritation at himself, no panic, no petulance.....

The film is scheduled for release in April.... And then will come true the dreams of Tom Naud and Frank Scott [the ballplayers' agent] and Mickey Mantle and Roger Maris. And of the Little Leaguer from Fort Lauderdale who sat on the bench in the dugout one day watching his heroes go through take after take of the same scene. "Would you want to be a movie star?" he was asked, in the fond delusion that he would respond like a true-blue, red-blooded, 100% all-American boy and say, no sir, he'd rather be a big league ballplayer.

"You bet," he said.

"Even after seeing all that stuff they have to go through?" he was asked.

"Sure," he said.

"Why, for Pete's sake?"

"You make a lot of money."

From SI: July 2, 1962

The Yankees' Desperate Gamble

by Walter Bingham

64

Mantle's legs had always been fragile, but by 1962, his health became a nearly daily concern for Yankee manager Ralph Houk. As this story by Walter Bingham indicates, the demands of a pennant race sometimes overruled the dictates of safety and Mantle was forced to play in extreme pain. But he did come back in '62, batting .321, hitting 30 home runs and leading the Yankees to their second consecutive World Series championship.

It was nothing less than a cold and ruthless gamble. Faced with a losing streak and the distasteful prospect of not winning the pennant for a change, the New York Yankees rushed the most valuable property in baseball back into action last week and ran the risk of losing him forever.

Mickey Mantle's legs had not yet healed, as anyone could see. He limped when he walked and staggered when he swung. He ran stiff-legged and he was unable, or afraid, to make turns. He was not, in short, ready....

It was undeniable that the Yankee brass had permitted Mantle to play before he had fully recovered. It was a decision made out of desperation. During the five weeks Mickey was out of the lineup, the Yankees were an ordinary team, winning and losing with fourth-place regularity. His value to the team had always been obvious. His absence had made it more so....

The Yankee attack all but stopped.... Roger Maris found that without Mantle batting behind him he saw few good pitches. One day he was walked five straight times, four of them intentional. After the game he phoned Mantle to check on his condition and urge him back. When Mantle did rejoin the team, still limping badly, it became a daily joke for Maris to say hopefully, "Looking great, Mick. You should be ready to play in two days, right?..."

What Mantle had done was tear a muscle—the adductor muscle, the doctor said later—in his right thigh, so that he could not straighten his leg. When he fell [while trying to beat out an infield single] he landed smack on his left knee, and as the weeks passed, it was this knee that bothered Mantle most. He suffers from an arrested case of osteomyelitis that began with

With his right thigh and left knee both injured, Mantle was forced to wince with every step.

a high school football injury, and both his knees are very tender. Even when he is healthy he limps, and this is why he must spend 10 minutes before every game wrapping each knee in long, wide strips of rubberized bandage....

Being unable to play himself, Mantle concentrated on rooting, keeping the Yankees laughing with his Oklahoma-style sense of humor....

At least 50 times a day, Mantle was asked about the condition of his legs. Finally he got a piece of paper on which he printed: "Slight improvement. Be back in two weeks. So don't ask." He taped the paper to his chest for all the world to see. "It won't work," he said gloomily as he put it on. "They'll still ask how's it feeling...."

One thing worries Mantle far more than his fragile knees and his baseball career, although it is a related problem. His father died of cancer at 39 and two uncles died of the same disease younger than that. "I hope I make it to 40," Mantle said recently. "Sure, I kid about it, but I think about it, too."

Mickey Mantle's medical prospects are of far more than personal interest... "We score more runs when he's in there," said [manager Ralph] Houk. "Everything is better when he's in there." That much is true. Houk also said: "He passed the first test with flying colors. That's a relief off my mind." This was for show. What Houk meant is that he is scared to death. He knows Mantle's condition is still far from good, and that without Mantle the world champion Yankees are goners.

From SI: June 17, 1963

For the Want of a Warning the Pennant Was Lost

by Robert W. Creamer

Yet another injury—this time a broken foot—sidelined Mantle in 1963, but the headline over Robert W. Creamer's story proved to be inaccurate: Even with Mantle playing in only 65 games, the Yankees won the pennant, though they were swept in four games by Sandy Koufax and the Los Angeles Dodgers in the World Series.

The Baltimore rain fell in a fine steady mist, as from a garden hose. You could see it only by watching it strike the puddles shuddering in front of the dugout or by looking at it glinting down past the upper stands.... The rain finally slowed and stopped, and the game started, more than an hour late. The night before, when Baltimore had

When Mantle went down again, the Yankee future looked as dark as the Baltimore night.

beaten New York 3–1 to take over the league lead, Mantle had hit a home run, two outfield flies and a single to center and had been on third base, waiting to score, when the game ended. Now, this wet night, he singled to right in the second inning and walked in the fourth. In the sixth he doubled to left and scored when Roger Maris hit a home run to put New York ahead 3–2.

Then in the last half of the sixth inning Brooks Robinson of Baltimore hit a ball high and far toward the centerfield fence. Mantle turned and raced back for it, running at full speed in his choppy, high-stepping sprinter's stride. He looked up over his right shoulder as he ran, and as he neared the ball he lifted his glove to catch it. But the point of juxtaposition of glove and ball that Mantle anticipated was theoretical—it lay a few feet beyond the seven-foot-high wire fence bounding the outfield. There was no cinder warning track in front of the fence, as in most ball parks, and as the ball went over for a home run Mantle ran into the fence. His left foot hit on the downward stroke of its stride, and his spikes caught in the wire mesh. The front part of his foot was bent violently up and back. The momentum of his run smashed him up against the fence and he seemed to hang there for an instant. Then he crumpled to the ground.

Roger Maris ran over to him and Bobby Richardson ran out and the players in the Yankee bullpen in right field streamed along the

fence toward him. Other players ran out and joined the uniformed throng massed incongruously in the deepest part of the outfield....

The stretcher went out and disappeared into the crowd. When it appeared again, it bore Mantle. He lay on his side, half sitting up, supporting himself on his right elbow, somber and quiet. "He looks like a warrior being carried on his shield," said [a writer] in the press box.

Beneath the stands in the corridors behind the Yankee dressing room the sportswriters were held at bay by polite but adamant guards. The writers argued. "You can't go in," a guard said flatly, and the writers waited. They saw New York players come back through the tunnel from the dugout—the Baltimore half of the inning had ended—and go into the dressing room: Ralph Terry, Bobby Richardson, Roger Maris, others. They looked tired. They were in the dressing room with Mantle for only a moment or two, and then filed back along the tunnel to the dugout. The game went on.

Beneath the stands a door opened and a wheeled stretcher rolled out. Mantle lay on it, flat on his back now, a blanket covering him. He was rolled quickly to an ambulance waiting in the dark at the curb outside the stadium. The stretcher was lifted and slid in. Mantle stared up at the dark ceiling of the ambulance, his face expressionless. Then he lifted his hands and pressed them there for a long moment. The ambulance drove away.

From SI: August 26, 1963

On the Trail of a Hero

by Ed Graham

As Ed Graham quickly learned when he spent 24 hours with the Yankee star in 1963, the easiest part of being Mickey Mantle was the baseball. In many ways Mantle was sport's first TV-generated mega-celebrity, the first to face the public's incessant demands upon his time and energy.

A rumor swept the airport lobby that the Yankee plane was about to land at Gate 2. A bus was already out on the field waiting to spirit the players away. Even at midnight in Kansas City, obviously a mob was anticipated.

The crowd rushed to Gate 2. After one person showed it could be done, we all poured through the gate and onto the airfield itself. Soon a light appeared in the west. It drew closer. A searchlight flicked on. With a roar the "Yankee Special" touched down and taxied to within 50 feet of us. A ramp was rolled up, the door burst open and down streamed the ballplayers, Cletis Boyer first. Swiftly they moved through a gauntlet of fans which extended from the base of the plane ramp to the door of the bus. The first Yankees signed autographs as they moved swiftly along.

Then Mantle appeared at the door of the plane. His crutches were gone now. As he came down, there was only a faint trace of the limp. A cheer went up. The gauntlet dissolved to reform in a circle at the base of the ramp. It swallowed Mantle up. He too began to sign, but the size of the crowd made it impossible for him to move as rapidly as the others....

Finally Mantle made it to the bus. The mass formed up again outside his window and began thrusting things in at him. He signed them quickly and seriously. I noticed that he was very much at ease with the kids. He admonished one who thrust the same piece of paper back in for a second autograph.... Suddenly there were loud shouts of "Look out!" "Stand back now!" "This bus is leaving!" The engine was gunned. The crowd shrieked and scattered, and the world champion baseball team rolled off into the night.

[At breakfast the following morning in Mantle's hotel room:]

"Do you always eat in your room?" I asked Mantle.

Mantle's non-stop autograph marathon began with some fans outside the team bus.

"He doesn't get to eat much if he goes downstairs," [Whitey] Ford answered.

The phone rang and Mantle answered it. He said, "Hello," then listened for what seemed a long time. "Well, I'll sign at the door," he said. "But they can't come in. It's Room 638." As Mantle hung up, Whitey Ford asked, "Who was that?" His tone indicated the great pitcher sensed trouble. Like any Yankee fan, I knew that Ford relied on an uncanny ability to outthink his opponents. Now I was seeing a touch of it here in the room.

"It was a fella," Mantle answered. "Said he's a friend of my brother Frank's. And he's got a couple of kids with him."

"You don't have a brother Frank," Ford said. Was this an old Abbott and Costello act they were putting on for my benefit? "I know I don't," Mickey said. "I figured the fella'd be embarrassed in front of the two kids and all."

There was a knock at the door. Mantle opened it and greeted two boys who wore Yankee caps. Each got an autograph and a handshake. Then the man led them away. Breakfast was resumed.

Within five minutes it struck. First screams down the hall. Then the tread of fast-running feet. The words "Room 638" could be heard amid the babble. Then suddenly there was pounding on the door. It grew more furious. Occasional bodies hurled themselves at the door. We actually seemed to be living a scene from Hitchcock's *The Birds*—the one in which millions of the tiny creatures pecked and hurled themselves at a door until they splintered the wood, burst through and pecked out the eyes of their victims inside.

I opened Ford's door [from the adjoining room] and told the kids they would have to leave. They ignored me. I told them Mantle's room was 738 (Mel Allen's). But they did not believe me. Some had fallen to the floor and were peeking under the door. "I can see his shoes!" one boy called up triumphantly. "Yeah, and they're moving!" another shouted....

Ralph Terry told Mantle and Ford that the bus was loading. The two of them plunged off into the sea of people—Ford in front, attempting to part it, with less spectacular results than Moses.

[Later, back at the hotel after the game:]

Riding up on the elevator ... I asked Mantle what his plans were for the night.

"I'm going to call my motel in Joplin. My wife said she might come up from Dallas. If she did I can get there in less than an hour. Otherwise I'm going to bed."

The door opened for the sixth floor. Mantle and I shook hands, and he left. As the elevator door closed, I heard a whoop and the now familiar stampede of feet. "It's Mickey Mantle!" kids shouted. "Hey, Mickey!"

It felt nice to be getting off on Ralph Houk's floor.

Even a glimpse of Mantle's shoes was enough to send his fevered fans into ecstasy.

From SI: September 28, 1964

Out in Front with a New Look

by William Leggett

During the latter years of his career, Mantle, with nothing left to prove, became looser and more relaxed and, ultimately, more able to handle the leadership role so many had tried to thrust upon him. In 1964, William Leggett examined the new Yankee generation and Mantle's critical contribution to the team chemistry. It would be Mantle's last big season as he batted .303, hit 35 homers and drove in 111 runs. He also took New York to the World Series, his twelfth in 14 seasons, where the Yankees lost to the St. Louis Cardinals in seven games.

These 1964 Yankees are not the heroic stoics that tradition makes them out to be. In action, the 1964 Yankees have been a phenomenon of collective ineptitude. Their hitting has been bad, their fielding spotty, their base running ragged, their relief pitching brutal. Devout Yankee haters and dedicated Yankee fans alike will admit that since April this team has been playing some very un-Yankeelike baseball.

There were notable signs of improvement last week, but no matter how this year finally ends for the Yankees, it is indisputable that there are some remarkable differences between this and former New York teams. Although vast internal shuffles have brought a new manager, a new general manager, a new road secretary, a new concessionaire and even new owners, the basic difference is that the Yankees have acquired a warm, human image. This has occurred because they have been beaten and forced to scramble hard for victories against teams that former Yankee clubs were able to shrug off.

It has been a new set of Yankees—Jim Bouton, Phil Linz, Joe Pepitone, Al Downing, Mel Stottlemyre, Pedro Ramos—that has been carrying the team through its last drive, and these Yankees have never been through a pennant drive before. True enough, there is an old Yankee leading the new ones on, trying to ease the pressures, trying to contribute more than he is physically capable of contributing. That, of course, is Mickey Mantle, and he has played this season with a quiet valor that has inspired every member of the team, the new set and the old hands. "The thing about Mantle this year," says relief pitcher Steve Hamilton, "is that you know he is playing with injuries that are tremendously painful. It's agony for all of us to watch him stumble in the outfield and try to swing a bat. But in watching

him you stop worrying about what's bothering *you*. You say to yourself, 'He's making $100,000 a year. He's famous and could retire right now just on his name. If he can do it, I can, too.' "

Mantle's sense of humor also has been a big factor. Time and again it has, by itself, lifted the whole team from mass dejection. "When Mantle says something that he thinks is funny," says Hamilton, "it always is. He waits for the right time. There are many players on this team with a sharper wit, but when Mickey says something, everybody laughs...."

When infielder Phil Linz, the man who has done more for the harmonica than anyone since Borrah Minevitch, was in the doghouse with Berra as well as general manager Ralph Houk and coach Frank Crosetti, it was Mantle who eased his mind about the whole harmonica incident. "Phil," Mantle said, "I read where you played 'Mary Had a Little Lamb' after we lost all those games in Chicago. It could have been a lot worse. You could have played 'Happy Days Are Here Again....' "

At the end of last week the new Yankees were in first place. Some old Yankees were there also, of course, and also responsible. Mickey Mantle, Elston Howard, Whitey Ford. Old and new—but different.

Mantle became the comic relief for new Yankees like Bouton (second from Mantle's left).

Mickey Mantle Day • Yankee Stadium • 1969

Mickey Mantle's decline paradoxically
began long before he reached his peak as a player.

The injuries that began in his rookie year ravaged him throughout his career and unquestionably shortened his days and nights on the diamond. His nights off the diamond didn't help either. Because of the early deaths of the men in his family, including his beloved father, he had a let's-eat-drink-and-be-merry-for-tomorrow-we-die attitude. His carousing with friends such as Billy Martin and Whitey Ford took its toll. So did his cavalier approach to corrective exercise. Instead of working to rehabilitate this knee or that thigh he'd shoot baskets instead.

Still, as Ford has pointed out, Mantle appeared in 2,401 regular-season games, 237 more than the Iron Horse, Lou Gehrig, and he and Gehrig were about the same age—Lou, 35, Mickey, 36—when physical deterioration forced them to retire.

Mantle didn't take care of himself but he played in the face of pain. His knees always hurt. His daily pre-game regimen included wrapping his bad legs in what seemed like miles of protective bandage. Yankee players still talk of his appearance in the 1961 World Series after he had been hospitalized late in the regular season with an aggravated abscess in his thigh. Because it had been lanced and the wound was still open, he sat out the first two games of the Series. But he played the third game, although blood was oozing from the wound, and he started again the next day. After he singled and ran to first base blood was seeping through his uniform. Reluctantly, he gave way to a pinch runner and played no more in the Series.

He came back the next season and won the MVP award despite more injuries, but he was wearing down. In three straight World Series—1961, '62 and '63—he did almost nothing at bat. He had his splendid revival in the 1964 Series (three homers, eight RBIs, eight runs scored), but that was his last Series and his last hurrah. His final four years as a player were feeble; there were memorable moments but not many. The Yankees were terrible, and Mantle wasn't much better. The outfield had become so difficult for him that he played first base his last two seasons.

There were no heartfelt goodbyes when he played his last game in 1968 because there was

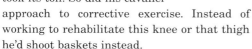

by Robert W. Creamer

hope he might try one more season. But he never played again. "I can't get around on the fast ball," he explained. He was remarkably upbeat about it, as he was about so many things in his life. Paradoxically, the country boy's big-city restaurant, Mickey Mantle's on Central Park South in New York City, went over big. He had his finger in many money-making pies in his post-baseball life and while a few didn't work out, most did. He made a lot of money and a lot of friends after he left baseball. Affection for him grew. TV interviews and film clips of him as a player helped polish his image as a decent, amiable man. He loved hitting home runs, for instance, but in the clips you could see that he didn't flaunt them, didn't gaze after them with self-admiration. Instead he seemed almost embarrassed, and as he trotted around the bases he kept his face tucked down toward his neck, as though hoping nobody would notice what he had done.

When his alcoholism and his terrible final illness became public the sins of the past were raked over, and some holier-than-thou critics castigated them. But for most people it was an idol that cancer crippled and death took, an idol and a friend who had given them a great deal of pleasure, a good guy, someone they had thoroughly enjoyed knowing, someone they would miss.

Mantle's biggest hit after his retirement was his restaurant in New York City.

From SI: June 21, 1965

Decline and Fall of a Dynasty

by Jack Mann

Early in the 1965 season, as the Yankees struggled, Sports Illustrated's Jack Mann examined the sources of their decline. His predictions of the end for the mighty Yankees proved absolutely accurate as New York finished in sixth place at 77–85, the team's first sub-.500 season since 1925. The precipitous fall paralleled the trajectory of Mantle's career, whose injuries became more and more crippling. He would never again hit 30 home runs, bat over .300 or drive in more than 80 runs. When he announced his retirement before the 1969 season, no one was surprised.

... The Yankees in battle array are suddenly no larger than life, and they are strange to behold in their present humble estate: just another good baseball team, certainly much better than their current second-division standing, but debilitated by age, crippled by injury and vulnerable to attack because their unwonted uncertainty makes them prone to manual and cerebral error.

The Yankees, like a fine old horse going on class and guts, may struggle home in third place, as they did after stumbling starts in 1940 and again in 1959. They could even, by a stretch of the imagination, win the pennant and the season would be saved. But the era—29 pennants and 20 World Championships in 44 years—would still be over. The Yankees will win again, maybe next year, but probably never again will they, or any team, dominate....

"They need four or five new men," says Ed Lopat, "and they just don't have them."

There's something else the Yankees no longer have. It has been fashionable expertise over the years to point out the Yanks' snug defense, their bench, the crafty pitching and the overall team effort. "When one guy was down," says Bill Skowron, who played on seven Yankee pennant winners before he was traded in 1962, "a couple of others would pick him up. But we was never as banged up as they are this year." They was never without a superstar, either. Lou Gehrig minded the store in the brief hiatus between Babe Ruth and Joe DiMaggio, and Mickey Mantle arrived the year DiMaggio was finishing up. In baseball they call it "the big guy," and the Yankees have always had one, at least since 1920.

"I ain't underrating Elston Howard," says

Billy Martin, "but there were years they wouldn't have won the pennant with five Howards if they didn't have Mickey." Mantle, the one-man orthopedic ward, is even more a symbol of the Yankees in crisis than he was in their predominance. He plays on, on agonized legs that would keep a clerk in bed, and the opposition wonders how. "He's hurting worse than ever," says John Blanchard, banished by the Yankees to Kansas City, "but he won't admit it."

"I don't see how the heck he can keep going," says Baltimore's Norm Siebern, another ex-Yankee. "It has to be his last year," an American League manager concluded after watching the 33-year-old Mantle for the first time this season. "He can't go on that way."

Following the Yankees these days is like watching a cowboys and Indians movie in which the bugle sounds but the cavalry never quite arrives. It is superstar time, but there is no superstar.

As the losses mounted and his performance became spottier, Mantle vented his frustration.

Mantle and Mays

by Ron Fimrite

In 1985, Commissioner Peter Ueberroth decided to reinstate Mickey Mantle and Willie Mays, both of whom had been prohibited from holding a salaried job in baseball in punishment for the relatively innocuous publicity jobs they had accepted with a pair of Atlantic City casinos. Their return to the game was cause for celebration and for this memorable story from Sports Illustrated's Ron Fimrite.

They had little boys' names—Mickey and Willie—but they were giants in their time, superstars before that word got contaminated by overuse. Mantle and Mays—names ingrained together in the sporting consciousness. Their lives and their careers are curiously parallel. They were born the same year, 1931. They arrived in the big leagues the same year, 1951, and in the same city, New York. They played the same position, centerfield. Both hit .300 or better 10 times and both hit more than 50 homers twice. And though their entire careers were spent in separate leagues, they did play against each other, in the 1951 and 1962 World Series.

They are both in baseball's Hall of Fame. And because they both took jobs with Atlantic City casinos as "ambassadors of goodwill," they were both prohibited from holding any salaried job in the game they so magnificently graced.

Prohibited, that is, until Monday afternoon when commissioner Peter Ueberroth welcomed back baseball's two prodigal sons with open arms. "They are two of the most beloved and admired athletes in the country today," says Ueberroth, "and they belong in baseball."

Mays had been the first to go. Commissioner Bowie Kuhn turned him out in 1979 when he went to work for Bally's Park Place Casino Hotel. Mays said he was "shocked." In 1983, when Del Webb's Claridge Casino Hotel decided it would be good business to have an immortal of its own on the payroll, it hired Mantle. Kuhn promptly banished him, too. "After what happened to Willie," Mantle said, he expected it. Neither complained publicly of his treatment, though both are delighted to be reinstated. Kuhn's reasoning in both instances had been that the two old ballplayers might well be

81

Both highly touted rookies, Mantle and Mays arrived in New York in the same year.

exposed to unsavory elements. Long after the 1919 Black Sox threw the World Series, Kuhn was terrified of anything that smacked too obviously of gambling. He was in no way dissuaded from his course by the knowledge that both Mantle and Mays hold jobs that get them no closer to gambling than the golf course and the banquet hall....

Even without the stigma of banishment, Mantle and Mays have had to endure what may seem to the rest of us the peculiar limbo life of the retired superstar. When we finally leave our jobs in that jungle out there, we are either at or approaching our dotage, but the athlete finishes in the prime of his life. In the years that follow he is forever reminded of the evanescence of all things. Coping with reminders of his increasingly distant past demands a gift not found on the playing field. What do you do with a boy's name when the boy's game is over?....

At 53 [Mantle] looks trim enough, his weight close to the 200 pounds or so he carried as a player. His hair has grown darker than it was in his brilliant blond youth and—oh, the passage of time—it is speckled with gray.... Once considered baseball's fastest runner, Mantle limps perceptibly when he walks now, the lega-

cy of four operations he has had on his fragile right knee....

[Driving home after a lengthy banquet:]

Mantle's head is resting back against the seat. Mention of [Ted] Williams' name seems to revive him.

"Greatest hitter I ever saw," he says.... "I didn't see them all, course, but to me he was the best."

"And not just a singles hitter," says [Bill] Dougall [of the Claridge hotel and casino], "like some of these guys with the high averages now. He hit the long ball, Mick. Like you."

"Like me?" Mantle says quietly in the darkness of the speeding car, his broad pale face illuminated by approaching headlights. "Why, he wasn't like me at all. He was a real hitter. I mean, he'd take that short swing of his and hit everything. Yeah, he hit some so hard they went over the fence. But he was a real hitter. Me, I just got up there and swung for the roof ever' time and waited to see what would happen. No, not like me. He wasn't like me."

The others watch silently as he falls fast asleep....

The Mantles have lived in [their] four-bedroom house [in the Preston Hollow section of Dallas] since 1957. "It's the best business deal I

In his retirement, Mantle gave freely of his time, as at this cancer fundraiser in 1985.

ever made," says Mantle, "and I had nothing to do with it. My wife, Merlyn, found it and bought it. She spells her name M-e-r-l-y-n. Yogi always thought her name was Marilyn and that, with my accent, I couldn't pronounce it right. I met her back in 1950. She was a senior then at Picher High. I graduated the year before from Commerce High in the next town over. The two schools were rivals, so I came back to watch them play football that year. Merlyn was a majorette. I tell her that when I first saw her she was prancin' around in front of a lot of people with her pants off. Friend of mine knew her sister and that's how we met...."

Mantle ... returns with a tall Styrofoam cup that has a photo on it of a sooty-faced teenage Mickey in a miner's helmet on one side, and on the other the legend DON'T WORRY ABOUT ME—I CAN ALWAYS GET A JOB. He turns the cup in his hand. "I worked in the lead mines outside of Commerce when I was a kid. They went straight down into the ground 400 feet, not into the side of some hill. I had to go down there. My father was the ground boss. Worked the mines all his life. He died when he was 39. Grandfather and uncles the same thing. Early. Hell, I only figured to live 'til 40. That's why I had as much fun as I could while I was young. You know the old saying, 'If I'd known I was gonna live this long, I'd a taken better care of myself.' That's me, all right."

From SI: April 18, 1994

Time in a Bottle

by Mickey Mantle with Jill Lieber

In late 1993, Mantle was forced to confront the demons of alcoholism that had been plaguing him for 40 years. Having finally hit rock bottom, he checked himself into the Betty Ford Center and began the painful process of constructing a life for himself that did not include drinking. In this wrenchingly candid first-person account, given to Sports Illustrated's Jill Lieber, Mantle told the world about his problem. Eighteen months later he was dead, gone just as his new life was getting started.

I began some of my mornings the past 10 years with the "breakfast of champions"—a big glass filled with a shot or more of brandy, some Kahlua and cream. Billy Martin and I used to drink them all the time, and I named the drink after us. Sometimes when I was in New York with nothing to do, and Billy and I were together, we would stop into my restaurant on Central Park South at around 10 in the morning, and the bartender would dump all the ingredients into a blender and stir it right up. It tasted real good.

Unfortunately for everybody else around me, one "breakfast of champions" and they could kiss the day goodbye. After one drink, I was off and running. And unless I had a business engagement, I'd often keep on drinking until I couldn't drink anymore....

I always took pride in my dependability when I was doing public-relations work, endorsements and personal appearances. I always wanted to do my best. It was when I had no commitments, nothing to do or nowhere to be that I lapsed into those long drinking sessions. It was the loneliness and emptiness. I found "friends" at bars, and I filled my emptiness with alcohol. In those instances I was almost totally out of it by early evening. I could hardly talk. I'd try to get somebody to go to dinner with me, and I'd start drinking vodka martinis. I'd order a meal, but I wouldn't eat. I'd just sit there and drink.

In the past five years I used alcohol as a crutch. To help me overcome my shyness and make me feel more comfortable before all those personal appearances, I'd warm up with three or four vodkas before leaving the hotel, go straight to the cocktail party and have three or

Even as early as 1960, the bottle was a nearly ubiquitous presence at Mantle's side.

four more drinks, and then I'd start feeling, Whew, all right. Let's go....

The older I got, and the more alcohol I drank, the more I had these weird hangovers—bad anxiety attacks.... It got to the point where I was worrying so much about everything—what was happening to my memory, how awful my body felt, how I hadn't been a good husband or a good father—that I was even afraid to be alone in the house. I'd ask my youngest son, Danny, to please stay at home with me. And there were times when I locked myself in the bedroom to feel safe....

Several times in recent years my friends and family had discussed intervention, but knowing how stubborn and hard-headed I was, they knew it wouldn't have worked. I needed to think that an alcohol-treatment program was *my* idea. Danny had checked himself into Betty Ford last October because he felt he was drinking too much. I asked Danny about the kinds of things that happen there. I don't talk much, and I wasn't sure I wanted to get into a situation at Betty Ford where I'd have to talk about my feelings. I was afraid I was going to cry in front of strangers, and I thought people would think

less of me. Mickey Mantle shouldn't cry....

When I came up with the Yankees in 1951, at age 19, I'd hardly ever had a drink. My father wouldn't have stood for me getting drunk. But the following spring, when Dad died of Hodgkin's disease at age 39, I was devastated, and that's when I started drinking. I guess alcohol helped me escape the pain of losing him....

Back then I could quit drinking when I went to spring training. I got myself into shape. Then when the season started I went back to drinking again—Billy, Whitey Ford and me. Hell, we played mostly night games. We'd be home by 1 a.m. and sleep until 9 or 10. I never used to have hangovers. I had an incredible tolerance for alcohol, and I'd always look and feel great in the morning. I don't think I ever blew a game because I was drunk or hung over. Maybe I hurt the team once or twice, but if I wasn't feeling right, I got myself out of the game early. When my dad died, Casey became like a father to me. He'd call me in sometimes and say, "Look, I know we don't have a curfew, but you're overdoing it a bit. Besides, it's not helping you any." I couldn't fool Casey....

Everybody tries to make the excuse that

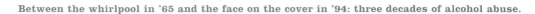

Between the whirlpool in '65 and the face on the cover in '94: three decades of alcohol abuse.

88

injuries shortened my career. Truth is, after I'd had a knee operation, the doctors would give me rehab work to do, but I wouldn't do it. I'd be out drinking. The first time I hurt my knee, in the '51 World Series, I was only 19. I thought, Hey, I'll be all right. I hurt my knees again through the years, and I just thought they'd naturally come back. Everything had always come natural to me. I didn't work hard at it. When the last World Series game was over, I didn't think about baseball until the spring. I blame that on stupidity.

After I retired, my drinking got really bad. I went through a deep depression. Billy, Whitey, Hank Bauer, Moose Skowron—I left all those guys, and I think it left a hole in me. I tried to fill it up by drinking. I still don't feel like I have much in common with a lot of people. But with those guys, I shared life. We were as close as brothers. I haven't met anybody else I've felt as close to....

Everywhere I went people wanted to hear all the old stories about Billy and Whitey and our wild times. That was part of the legend of Mickey Mantle. Everybody just expected me to start drinking. They'd buy me drinks. I think they expected me to get drunk. It was like this: Mickey Mantle couldn't hit it out of the park anymore, but he could still drink 'em under the table.

I'd never thought about anything serious in my life for a continuous period of days and weeks until I checked into the Betty Ford Center for my 32-day stay. I've always tried to avoid anything emotional—anything controversial,

anything serious—and I did it through the use of alcohol. Alcohol always protected me from reality. But at Betty Ford, I could be myself. I wasn't Mickey Mantle. I was the guy in room 202.

When you first get to Betty Ford, you have to open up to the members of your dorm unit in group therapy sessions. It took me a couple of times before I could talk without crying. You're supposed to say why you're there, and I said because I had a bad liver and I was depressed. Whenever I tried to talk about my family, I got all choked up. One of the things I really screwed up, besides baseball, was being a father. I wasn't a good family man. I was always out, running around with the guys. Mickey Jr. could have been a helluva athlete. If he'd had *my* dad, he could have been a major league baseball player. My kids have never blamed me for not being there. They don't have to. I blame myself....

I feel like I'm the reason that Danny went to Betty Ford last fall. For all those years I'd make him go to lunch and dinner with me. I'd get Mickey Jr. and my next oldest son, David, to go too. I'd say, "Hey, what are you guys doing tonight? Let's go eat." Which would mean, "Let's go drink." They all drank too much because of me. We don't have normal father-son relationships. When they were growing up, I was playing baseball, and after I retired I was too busy traveling around being Mickey Mantle. We never played catch in the backyard. But when they were old enough to drink, we became drinking buddies. When we were together, it kind of felt like the old days with Billy and Whitey. I had no idea that I was making my kids drink like that....

My biggest disappointment in life was not being able to help my third son, Billy, who was named after Billy Martin. When he was only 19, Billy came down with Hodgkin's—the disease that killed my father, my father's father and Dad's two brothers—and I've always wished I'd been the one to get cancer, not Billy. Watching your kids suffer is unbearable.... Billy's Hodgkin's went into remission several times, but he led an unhappy life.... Within weeks after I got out of Betty Ford— and only two days after his mother had checked him into a rehab center in Wilmer, Texas—Billy had a heart attack and died. He was only 36.... If only I'd gone to Betty Ford sooner, Billy might still be here. If I hadn't been drinking, I might have been able to get him to stop doing drugs.

During my preadmission interview, I told the counselor that I drank because of depression that came from feeling I'd never fulfilled my father's dreams. I had to write my father a letter and tell him how I felt about him. You talk about sad. It only took me 10 minutes to write the letter, and I cried the whole time, but after it was over, I felt better. I said that I missed him, and I wished he could've lived to see that I did a lot better after my rookie season with the Yankees. I told him I had four boys—he died before

my first son, Mickey Jr., was born—and I told him that I loved him. I would have been better off if I could have told him that a long time ago....

I like the idea of having to stay sober in public, knowing that people are watching me. Now they won't be buying me drinks. They'll expect me *not* to drink. For all those years I lived the life of somebody I didn't know. A cartoon character. From now on, Mickey Mantle is going to be a real person.

I still can't remember much of the last 10 years, but from what I've been told, I really don't want those memories. I'm looking forward to the memories I'll have in the next 10 years.

In the end Mantle was prepared to face his demons with courage and dignity.

From SI: August 21, 1995

Mickey Mantle

by Richard Hoffer

*With Mantle's death, on August 13, 1995, came
the effort to understand his enduring hold on
the nation's affections. Sports Illustrated's
Richard Hoffer offered this provocative essay
on Mantle as man and myth.*

Mickey Mantle, with his death at 63, passes
from these pages forever and becomes the property of anthropologists, people who can more
properly put the calipers to celebrity, who can
more accurately track the force of personality.
We can't do it anymore, couldn't really do it to
begin with. He batted this, hit that. You can look
it up. Hell, we do all the time. But there's nothing in our library, in all those numbers, that
explains how Mantle moves so smoothly from
baseball history into national legend, a country's touchstone, the lopsided grin on our society.

He wasn't the greatest player who ever lived,
not even of his time perhaps. He was a center-
fielder of surprising swiftness, a switch-hitter of
heart-stopping power, and he was given to spec-
tacle: huge home runs (his team, the New York
Yankees, invented the tape-measure home run

for him); huge seasons (.353, 52 HRs, 130 RBIs
to win the Triple Crown in 1956); one World
Series after another (12 in his first 14 seasons).
Yet, for one reason or another, he never became
Babe Ruth or Joe DiMaggio—or, arguably, even
Willie Mays, his exact contemporary.

But for generations of men, he's the guy, has
been the guy, will be the guy. And what does
that mean exactly? A woman beseeches Mantle, who survived beyond his baseball career
as a kind of corporate greeter, to make an
appearance, to surprise her husband. Mantle
materializes at some cocktail party, introduc-
tions are made, and the husband weeps in the
presence of such fantasy made flesh. It means
that, exactly.

It's easy to account, at least partly, for the
durability and depth of his fame: He played on
baseball's most famous team during the game's
final dominant era. From Mantle's rookie season
in 1951—the lead miner's son signed out of
Commerce, Oklahoma, for $1,100—to his injury-
racked final year in 1968, baseball was still the
preeminent game in the country. This was

Taken in 1961, this timeless image could have come from any of Mantle's 12 trips to the Series.

baseball B.C. (Before Cable), and a nation's attention was not scattered come World Series time. Year in, year out, men and boys in every corner of the country were given to understand during this autumnal rite that there really was only one baseball team and that there really was only one player: No. 7, talked with a twang, knocked the ball a country mile. But it was more than circumstance that fixed Mantle in the national psyche; he did hit 18 World Series home runs, a record, over the course of 65 of the most watched games of our lives.

Even knowing that, acknowledging the pinstriped pedigree, the fascination still doesn't add up. If he was a pure talent, he was not, as we found out, a pure spirit. But to look upon his youthful mug today, three decades after he played, is to realize how uncluttered our memories of him are. Yes, he was a confessed drunk; yes, he shorted his potential—he himself said so. And still, looking at the slightly uplifted square jaw, all we see is America's romance with boldness, its celebration of muscle, a continent's comfort in power during a time when might did make right. Mantle was the last great player on the last great team in the last great country, a postwar civilization that was booming and confident, not a trouble in the world.

Of course, even had he not reflected the times, Mantle would have been walking Americana. His career was storybook stuff, hewing

more to our ideas of myth than any player's since Ruth. Spotted playing shortstop on the Baxter Springs Whiz Kids, he was delivered from a rural obscurity into America's distilled essence of glamour. One year Mantle is dropping 400 feet into the earth, very deep into Oklahoma, to mine lead on his father's crew, another he's spilling drinks with Whitey Ford and Billy Martin at the Copa.

A lesson reaffirmed: Anything can happen to anybody in this country, so long as they're daring in their defeats and outsized in victory. Failure is forgiven of the big swingers, in whom even foolishness is flamboyant. Do you remember Mantle in Pittsburgh in the 1960 Series, twice whiffing in Game 1 and then, the next day, crushing two? Generations of men still do. The world will always belong to those who swing from the heels.

Still, Mantle's grace was mostly between the lines; he developed no particular bonds beyond his teammates, and he established no popularity outside of baseball. As he was dying from liver cancer, none of the pre-tributes remarked much on his charm. And, as he was dying from a disease that many have presumed was drinking-related, there was a revisionist cast to the remembrances. Maybe he wasn't so much fun after all.

But, back then, he most certainly was. Drunkenness had a kind of high-life cachet in the '50s: It was manly, inasmuch as you were a stand-up guy who could be counted on to perform the next afternoon, and it was glamorous. Down the road, as Mantle would later confess from the other side of rehabilitation, it was merely stupid. But palling around with Billy and Whitey—just boys, really, they all had little boys' names—it amounted to low grade mischief. Whatever harm was being done to families and friends, it was a small price to pay for the excitement conferred upon a workaday nation.

In any event, we don't mind our heroes flawed, or even doomed. Actually, our interest in Mantle was probably piqued by his obvious destiny, the ruin he often foretold. As a Yankee he was never a whole person, having torn up his knee for the first first time in his first World Series in '51. Thereafter, increasingly, he played in gauze and pain, his prodigal blasts heroically backlit by chronic injury. But more: At the hospital after that '51 incident, Mantle learned that his father, Mutt, admitted to the same hospital that same day, was dying of Hodgkin's disease. It was a genetic devastation that had claimed every Mantle male before the age of 40. The black knowledge of this looming end informed everything Mickey did; there was little time, and every event had to be performed on a grand scale, damn the consequences. Everything was excused.

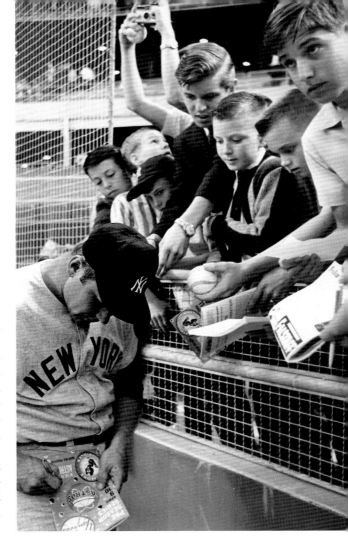

Signing autographs was as much a part of Mantle's daily routine as the stuff between the lines.

As we all know, having participated in this gloomy death watch, it didn't end with that kind of drama. It was Billy, the third of Mantles' four sons, who came down with Hodgkin's, and who later died of a heart attack at 36. Mickey lived much longer, prospering in an era of nostalgia, directionless in golf and drinking, coasting on a fame that confounded him (Why was this man, just introduced to him, weeping?).

Then Mantle, who might forever have been embedded in a certain culture, square-jawed and unchanged, did a strange thing. Having failed to die in a way that might have satisfied mythmakers, he awoke with a start and checked himself into the Betty Ford Center. This was only a year and a half ago, and, of course, it was way too late almost any way you figure it. Still, his remorse seemed genuine. The waste seemed to gall him, and his anger shook the rest of us.

The generation of men who watched him play baseball, flipped for his cards or examined every box score must now puzzle out the attraction he held. The day he died there was the usual rush for perspective and the expected sweep through the Yankee organization. They said the usual things. But former teammate Bobby Murcer reported that he had talked to the Mick before he had gone into the hospital the final time— neither a liver transplant nor chemotherapy could arrest the cancer or stop his pain—and Mantle, first thing, asked how a fund-raiser for children affected by the Oklahoma City bombing was going, something he and Murcer, also from Oklahoma, were involved in. It was odd, like the sudden decision to enter rehab and rescue his and his family's life, and it didn't really square with our idea of Mantle.

But let's just say you were of this generation of men, that you once had been a kid growing up in the '50s, on some baseball team in Indiana, and you remember stitching a No. 7 on the back of your KIRCHNER'S PHARMACY T-shirt, using red thread and having no way of finishing off a stitch, meaning your hero's number would unravel indefinitely and you would have to do it over and over, stupid and unreformed in your idolatry. And today here's this distant demigod, in his death, taking human shape. What would you think now?

95

Mantle, the symbol of a confident and untroubled nation: Is that the image which will persist?